A Matter of Conscience

Anne Packer with

Paul Knowles

Interim Publishing Co. Ltd., Toronto

Packer, Anne
  A Matter of Conscience

ISBN 0-9692988-1-1

1. Packer, David. 2. Conscience. 3. Abortion – Religious
aspects. 4. Police – Ontario – Toronto – Discipline. 5. Police
– Ontario – Toronto – Biography. I Knowles, Paul. II. Title.

HV7911.P32P3 1988   363.2'2   C88-095335-7

Published by Interim Publishing Co. Ltd.
53 Dundas Street East, Suite 306
Toronto, Ontario M5B 1C6
(416) 368-0250

Dedicated to Helen Burnie

Introduction

by Father Ted Colleton, C.S. Sp.

When Jim Hughes handed me the manuscript of "A Matter of Conscience" he said, "Anne would like you to write the introduction." I felt very honoured but was also very busy. I said, "Do I have to read the whole manuscript?" Jim said, "No, you know the story. Just read a FEW chapters" – he suggested them – "and that will give you enough to go on." That night, when I got into bed, I decided to glance over the manuscript and glean a few ideas. At 1 a.m. I was still reading and hadn't skipped a word. I reluctantly put it on the bedside table as I had to rise early. Before the next night I had completed the manuscript and wished there were more.

The main subject of the story is, of course, David Packer's courageous refusal to guard the Morgentaler "clinic" in which – to quote him – "babies are being killed every day." But there is far more to it than that. In a patently sincere and unpretentious way, Anne Packer, David's wife, traces the events that led to that momentous decision. She takes us to England where a young American nurse met a young Cambridge student – who was paying his fees by working as an orderly in the same hospital. Their first contact – separately – with abortion in the hospital makes frightening and absorbing reading. Their "courtship", engagement and ultimate marriage make a fascinating tale. Like so many marriages it was not all plain sailing. Anne tells the story with refreshing candor and both the "storms" and the eventual "calm seas" could be of considerable help to young couples who are experiencing similar difficulties.

The section concerning David's struggle with his conscience and his eventual victory over the temptation to "take the easy way out" will, I believe, make every reader take a long look in the mirror of his or her soul. We usually look back over the centuries to find our heroes and the models who help to mould our lives. In Constable David Packer we have a man who is "one of ourselves" – an ordinary man who took an extraordinary stand in defence of the lives of countless unborn babies. More than two centuries ago an Irish statesman named Edmund Burke in the British House of Parliament made a statement which has defied the corroding ravages of time – "All that evil needs in order to flourish is that good men do nothing." In "A Matter of Conscience" we read the gripping story of a quiet and unassuming man who, by force of circumstances not of his own making, was faced with a challenge which would change his life. He grasped the challenge with both hands and, in so doing, has changed the lives of more people than he will ever meet.

Contents

Chapter One

Fantastic

I suppose that it doesn't make a lot of sense. My husband had just told me that he had been charged with insubordination, and would probably lose his job as a police officer — the only job he had ever known.

And all I could think was, "Fantastic!!!"

It's not that I'm one of those police wives you read about — frightened every time my husband walks out the door in uniform, jumping whenever the phone rings when he's on duty, scared to death that the worst has just happened. Somehow, I've been able to treat his job as "just another job."

I knew that David enjoyed being a police officer. But as he stood in the doorway to our little home in New Toronto, and I looked down into his eyes from where I stood on the stairs, holding a basket of laundry, my first reaction was, "Fantastic."

David's a good cop. He had never caused trouble in the department, and anyone who knows him would insist that David Packer is a very unlikely person to challenge orders, foment discord, or initiate a mutiny. That isn't his style.

My husband is a quiet man, a man who prefers solitude to crowds, an evening at home to a night on the town, time with his family to nights out with "the boys." His record as a policeman was excellent. He had received a couple of minor criticisms for the kind of slips that happen to almost any cop, things like showing up late for a court case, but disciplinary action was very foreign to him.

He was more likely to receive commendations — and most likely to generally be completely overlooked by his superiors as he just did his job, day in and day out.

He had also been honoured for bravery for the time when he put his life on the line to save a child from a burning apartment.

This time, he had put his livelihood on the line for his conscience, and for the lives of other children, unborn babies who were being killed, every day.

My husband, Police Constable David Packer, had been charged with insubordination because he refused to guard the illegal abortuary run by Henry Morgentaler.

The official charge reads, "David John Packer, Police Constable 1512, you stand charged that you did without lawful excuse, disobey, omit or neglect to carry out a lawful order...and did thereby commit a major offence." The incident that led to David being charged occurred on April 8, 1987. It has changed the direction of our lives ever since.

The police charge sheet outlines the charge this way: "Being a member of the Metropolitan Toronto Police Force, attached to the Number 14 Division, you, on Wednesday, April 8th, 1987, were working the 7:30 a.m. to 5:30 p.m. relief, assigned to Zone 2 South, Court at 10:00 a.m. and the Morgentaler Clinic at 12 Noon. At about 12:30 p.m. you had conversation with Staff Sergeant Alan Griffiths, relative to your duties at the Morgentaler Clinic.

"At this time you advised Staff Sergeant Alan Griffiths you could not stand by a place that was killing babies; the detail was not a lawful order, and you would not do it. At about 12: 59 p.m. in the presence of Sergeant Alexander Crawford, Staff Sergeant Alan Griffiths gave you a direct order to attend outside the Morgentaler Clinic to which you replied, "I respectfully refuse. I don't think it's a lawful order."

"At about 1:05 p.m., in the presence of Staff Sergeant Alan Griffiths, Superintendent John Getty ordered you to perform the duty detailed to you by Staff Sergeant Alan Griffiths at the Morgentaler Clinic to which you replied, "I must respectfully decline."

"Without lawful excuse you disobeyed a lawful order."

David pleaded not guilty to the charge. However, he was found guilty by a police tribunal, appealed his conviction and, as I write this almost a year and a half later, is on limited duty with the Metropolitan Toronto police department, awaiting the result of that appeal.

April 8 started out as an ordinary day, the kind of day on duty that David had known ever since he joined the Metro police force, 10 years ago. David said nothing to me about his possible assignments that day, although he knew that he was likely to be given the job of guarding the abortuary since he was assigned to community foot patrol at his division, 14 Division. Foot patrol is a rotating duty that includes assignment to the Morgentaler clinic on Harbord Street in Toronto, and he had known that he was likely to be sent to Harbord Street since he joined the community foot patrol, in mid-March.

When orders were handed out that morning, at 7:30 a.m., he was told he had court duty until about noon, and then his afternoon shift would be spent at the "clinic."

I didn't know about this at the time. I also didn't know that David had already spent four shifts at the Morgentaler establishment, three on night duty when there was no activity inside, and one during the day when women were arriving to have abortions.

We had talked, very briefly, about what he might do if he was assigned duty at the abortuary. I remember a very short conversation, to which I contributed three words: "Don't do it."

I had already joined demonstrations in front of the "clinic," protesting against the killing of unborn children that was carried out, every day, in that place of death.

It's important to remember that, at that time, the "clinic" was operating illegally. As I write, there is no abortion law at all in Canada (and I pray that a law protecting our unborn brothers and sisters will eventually be passed), but then, the law clearly stated that what was going on inside was illegal. However, the powers that be in the province of Ontario had chosen to take no action against Morgentaler, because he had been acquitted of charges of procuring an abortion.

I'm not saying that if the law had stated that the "clinic" was perfectly legal, David should have done anything different from what he did — just because the law allows the killing of babies, as it has in hospitals for years, doesn't mean the law is right. Such a law would clearly be wrong. Doctors are still killing babies, and it is a horrible act, a crime against God and humanity, even if the Canadian Criminal Code doesn't have its morality straight on this issue. I'll come back to this in later chapters.

As I said, David had already accepted duty at the "clinic" during one other day shift. He told me later that he stood, on duty and in uniform, and watched a young girl and an older woman walk into the building. At that moment, he said, he felt like he was descending into hell.

He knew that he wasn't an innocent party any more. He now shared the responsibility for the horror that was taking place inside. He was there to make sure that girl could freely walk into that building, and then kill the baby that she carried in with her, inside her womb. And he was just sitting outside, doing nothing about it. In fact, most of his job consisted of preventing people who were opposed to abortion — as he was — from doing anything to prevent the killing.

He didn't talk to me about that experience. But he mulled it over and over inside, and had a lot of trouble sleeping.

On the night of April 7, the evening before he was to return to duty at the "clinic," he tossed and turned all night. He was ashamed that he had ever accepted those previous assignments at the abortuary. And he knew his conscience was making some demands on him — demands he would much rather have ignored.

The police department insists that police officers are essential at the "clinic" to keep the peace. There are frequently protesters there, including, on occasion, me — as I said, I had demonstrated in front of the "clinic" a number of times — and sometimes there were acts that are legally termed "trespassing". Protesters have chained the gates to the property closed, and registered their opposition to the abortions taking place inside in a number of ways that the authorities believed were outside the law.

David does not accept the rationale that his primary role at the "clinic" was, in reality, to keep the peace. He — and lots of other officers who have never stepped forward or taken the kind of action that David has — understand that their real role is to guard the Morgentaler abortuary. There's a world of difference between keeping the peace, and protecting a place where blatantly illegal activities are taking place, activities that are costing the lives of innocent human beings. Protecting people who are freely carrying out criminal activities should never be the role of a police officer.

The top brass of the Metro police department disagree with this view of officers' duties at the abortuary, of course.

So, David felt ashamed. He lay in our double bed, troubled and, for quite a while, frightened. I think he was equally afraid of what he would have to do, and of how he would live with himself if he didn't do it. I have to confess that I am a very sound sleeper, and I was unaware of the kind of mental and emotional anguish my husband was going through that night.

But sometime, in the wee hours of the morning, something changed. Something wonderful happened. Suddenly, he found the courage to refuse assignment to the Morgentaler "clinic" the next time it came his way. I really believe that God helped him at that moment.

The next morning, he was given the assignment to go to court and, when court was over, to report to the "clinic." Even then, David was hoping the issue would never come to a confrontation. Court duty often went overtime, and there was every chance that he would be sitting in a courtroom all day, waiting through some complicated legal wrangle, while someone else walked the beat at the abortuary.

It was not to be.

Court did go overtime, but only by about half an hour. David found himself walking back into 14 Division about 12:30 p.m.

He describes his return to the station as an act that he was watching, not doing, himself. He says it was as if his feet were carrying him into the station without any willful act on his part.

All of a sudden his feet had carried him in to stand before Staff Sergeant Griffiths, and David was telling his superior that he could not do the duty to which he had been assigned. I don't mean to say he was a robot or something like that, but somehow he found the kind of courage that I don't think he had before.

I'm very moved as I write about this. I realize that this must have been a very difficult thing for him to do, perhaps the toughest thing he ever did in his life. There's something about David's personality that makes it easier for him to be a hero in the face of a fire or other kind of disaster than it is for him to confront another person on a disagreement of this kind.

And while there was a slight chance that some way out might be found, even after he asked to be relieved of duty at the abortuary, I know he was sure he would be facing disciplinary action, that he would be in very big trouble with the police department, a department he had faithfully and loyally served for a decade.

And David's a very shy person. Having to face those men, his superior officers, and tell them he couldn't do what they were ordering him to do, was a more difficult assignment than any he had had as a cop, tougher than he will ever be able to explain.

There are several elements to those conversations with the superior officers that are not included in the charge sheet that carried David before the police tribunal, and that may well mean the end of his career. According to the police charges, he told his superior officers that, "I respectfully refuse. I don't think it's a lawful order."

Well, a lot had gone on before that statement. He told his sergeant that he could not guard the abortuary as a matter of conscience. David was, even then, not seeking a confrontation, although he was well aware that was a distinct possibility. Instead, he initially asked if he could be assigned to some other duty, and told the sergeant that he would be willing to do anything else that afternoon.

That was not the way it was to happen. David was asked to meet with higher ranking officers, and he knew, as he walked into the office for his "last chance," that this was not going to be quietly swept under the official carpet.

There are a lot of unspoken laws and rules in a police department. One of these is, when something official is to be carried out, officers who may have been working in shirt sleeves and bare heads will don full uniform before making any statements.

As David walked into the office of Superintendent John Getty, the superintendent and the staff sergeant were both in full uniform, and wearing their hats. David knew immediately that he would be charged for his refusal to guard the abortuary. He was; he was then ordered to appear before a police tribunal on the charge of disobeying a lawful order — insubordination.

I knew nothing about all that was taking place. David did not call me, nor did anyone else. He came home at the regular time, walked through our little foyer, and stopped at the foot of the stairs, looking up at me.

It was then I knew that something had happened, but I could never have guessed what it was. David didn't seem depressed, or unhappy. He was very calm and easygoing. That's what he's like most of the time, anyway, and I think that the courage that God had given him in the preceding hours was still holding him up. In fact, the David I know and love still has that kind of God-given courage. That courage is what has carried us through the last year and a half.

I stopped about halfway down the stairs, but before I could ask him what was going on, he said, "I refused to guard Morgentaler's, and I've been charged."

I said, "Good for you. Fantastic." I think my response was so positive because God was also working in me, giving me the immediate courage and calmness that I needed at that moment.

I suppose it would have been more normal to think, "Oh, no ! Help! What's going to happen now? We've got five growing kids, I'm a full-time mother, and David's income is all we have! David, we're in trouble! What have you done?", but none of those thoughts went through my mind at that moment.

Instead, I felt a great flood of relief and joy. What an opportunity God had given David! To stand and face evil, and say, "No, I will not be a part of this."

I was incredibly proud of David. I felt great. I knew that he had done a great thing.

That night, David slept like a baby.

Chapter Two

Different Worlds

David and I were born and raised worlds apart. I guess you'd have to say that the odds against our ever meeting were pretty high. The odds against the two of us ever having a chance to do something that could make a difference to thousands of lives — a chance I believe we now have — were absolutely out of sight.

David comes from a quaint little English town named Worminghall, near Oxford. It's about as far removed from Metro Toronto as anyone could possibly get.

I was born in Brooklyn, New York. Which is about as far from Worminghall as you can get.

David's father, Clifford Packer, is a bricklayer and carpenter, the sort of jack-of-all-trades that you'd love to be able to find in Toronto when you need your plumbing repaired, some shelves installed, or your chimney restored. He can do absolutely anything in that field. The family included David's mother, Janet, and his only sister, Margaret, who is ten years older than my husband.

From everything he tells me about it, he had an idyllic childhood, the kind of growing-up where you do all the things you would do if you didn't have a television. They didn't have a boob tube, but no one missed it. Instead, David had a fishing-and-swimming hole, where he played all the time with the local kids.

I mean, **all** the local kids — it was the kind of small village where everybody knew everybody. They still do.

Not too long ago, David sat down and wrote about some of his memories of his childhood in England. He wrote:

"Worminghall offered very few choices to its native sons — a bit of school, then the factory; a bit of school, then the farm; a bit of school, then a general laborer.

"For fun, the village kids would copy down the licence plates of cars passing through. Nobody owned a car in the village, so any car was just passing through. On a good day, we would get twenty. On bad days, we would give up after three or four hours to steal apples or assemble a bicycle of our scrounged scrap parts.

"Life in the tiny hamlet of Worminghall was as happy as any life could be. Poor, we lacked for nothing. Only the better-off newcomers to the village were aware of being hard up.

"Looking back, I remember not one unhappy day. Honestly.

"Only now that I have children do I realize how much my parents went without, just to keep us in school uniforms. And I suppose that the key point about my early life in Worminghall is that I got out. At the ripe old age of eleven I passed a school board exam that wrenched me as irrevocably from the companionship of my friends as any tooth has been ripped from its nurturing gum."

One thing his childhood did not include was any ongoing involvement with church. Like many English people, David was nominally an Anglican, but he would have been hard-pressed to tell you what an Anglican believed, or was supposed to believe.

I think David became a more solitary person when he was sent away to grammar school, at age 12. His school was quite far from home, and he had little contact with his fishing-hole friends. But while he became a more private person, he excelled in some academic areas. He was especially good at languages, a talent that he continues to use to this day.

Many of his duties with the Metro Toronto police department have made use of his facility with foreign languages, and, before the tribunal and his subsequent appeal removed him from duty on the street, David was learning Vietnamese, hoping to be able to work in the large and growing Vietnamese community in this city.

His academic abilities gained him entrance to the prestigious Cambridge university. That was a shock to his family. No Packer had ever gone on to post-secondary education before. Their name comes from the trade originally plied by his ancestors — they were wool packers — and the family had continued in those humble ways for many years.

He studied at Cambridge for two years. Then he met me, and his downfall began!

To pay his way through university, David was working at a hospital, as an orderly. There, he met two American nurses who had come to England to learn to be midwives.

Actually, I had come to England largely because a man I thought I was in love with had moved across the Atlantic from the United States. In fact, we had broken up, but I was convinced that following him to the British Isles might bring about a reconciliation. But only two weeks after I arrived in Great Britain — he was in Scotland, and I hadn't even seen him yet — I received a letter from this erstwhile love-of-my-life, informing me that he was engaged to some-one else.

That sort of information tends to put a damper on a passionate relationship. So when I encoun-tered a quirky but interesting orderly, I was free.

I'm not sure David really knew what he was getting into, when he began to court me. I come from Ukrainian, Irish and German stock — my parents are Otto and Elizabeth Fredericks — and I was an American city girl.

I was born in Brooklyn, New York, and spent the first few years of my life in that huge urban area. We moved around a bit, and I lived in Flushing, N.Y. and then in a place called New City, N.Y., a little farther removed from the met-ropolitan centre. My father found living there to be a little difficult. He worked for the phone com-pany, and had to commute a long way every day to get to work in the city.

I guess he decided that if he was going to take his family out of the city, he would go all the way. When I was a young girl, we moved to New Hampshire, about 300 miles from New York. I found myself transplanted into a small town called Warner, about half an hour from New Hampshire's capital city, Concord.

I went to school in Warner until grade eight, but then my devout Roman Catholic mother, with my grandmother's financial assistance, en-rolled me in a Catholic high school. The nearest one was in Concord, so it was in Concord that I spent all four of my high school years.

Unlike David's family, mine was religious. My mother has always had a strong faith, cradled as she was in a family blessed with many religious vocations. My father, on the other hand, while a baptized Catholic, has only recently come to understand how much God loves him. The Lord's love has also proved irresistible for my brothers Steven, Tom and his wife Pauline, Joe, and my sister Jean and her husband Michael.

Almost everything we did as a family involved our Roman Catholic faith in some way or another. Family vacations always meant a trip to New York. I really looked forward to them. Every April, we would go with our mother to visit with my grandparents in their semi-detached house in Brooklyn, and my paternal grandparents in Manhattan's east side.

Those visits always involved lots of parties. Although my mother's Dad was awfully shy, grandma was exactly the opposite. She was very outgoing, and a feminist ahead of her time. She worked outside the home, and was a musician, playing the organ all over the city.

My grandmother loved people. She worked with the visually handicapped, driving them on shopping trips and errands. She hosted lots of parties — some of my fondest memories as a child come from the parties at grandma's house.

Those two people were so different, one from the other. But they had a common bond that held them tightly together — their devout Roman Catholic faith, their belief in God and their moral code.

Their faith was shared by my mother, and by most members of their family. My grandfather's brother, Uncle Al, became a priest, and he established the first Catholic institution ministering to seamen.

15

That's not too surprising, because grandpa's family was raised in a most unusual situation — home to him, his parents and seven brothers and sisters, was a barge on the Erie canal. They must have invented express lines in grocery stores, because the children would often do the shopping by jumping off the moving barge at one bridge, running madly to a store, buying whatever goods they needed on the barge, and meeting the barge at the next bridge.

There are stories about children hanging off bridges almost missing the boat, but they all survived that unique childhood. And Uncle Al carried his love for ships into his ministry as a Catholic priest.

My Aunt Mary became a Maryknoll nun. Her greatest wish was to be a missionary teacher in China, or Japan, but she was very sickly, and unable to go to a foreign country. Instead, she carried out her vocation as a telephone operator at the Maryknoll convent. She willingly offered up her dreams to serve God in that apparently mundane way. She did a job that seemed small and menial, but she did it for God and with great love. The other sisters loved her very much, and although she is now dead, I still see her as a wonderful example.

I remember going to Maryknoll when I was a little girl. The nuns all wore the habit at that time, and it always seemed to me as though they just glided by me, exuding a sense of peace. That particular visit took place in the fall, as apples were being harvested in the orchard. I saw all the nuns up in the trees, picking apples, and in their habits, it looked as if they had glided there, too.

My Aunt Julia was also a nun. She belonged to the Josephite teaching order, and taught high school in New York for many years. She had a wonderful sense of humor, and was very kind and patient.

It's not too surprising that I remember a happy childhood in which religion and faith were simply part of normal life.

Two of my mother's brothers became priests. Uncle Joe is a Maryknoll missionary who has served in Guatemala, Japan and now Mexico, and Uncle Gene, who died just a year ago, was a high school teacher.

But despite all of this positive, faithful influence, despite my training in a Catholic high school and faithful attendance at church, I actually knew very little of personal faith. It took a crisis in my marriage to David before I actually came to know what faith in God really meant.

As a child, church was important to me because it was important to my mother, and I loved my mother desperately. But I don't think I really had a personal commitment to it. Otherwise, I would never have gone away from it, and the sad truth is, it didn't take me long, once I was away from home, to wind up very far away from church involvement. I quickly abandoned any commitment I had ever felt.

Maybe that was normal. It certainly seems to be the case with a lot of people when they get away from home.

For me, it happened when I returned to New York to go to nursing school. Although I had been born in Brooklyn, by the time I returned to the Big Apple to go to school, I had absorbed a lot of "small-town" atmosphere. At my nursing school, I was the student who had come the farthest from home, and I was only 17 years old.

At first, I hung around with a group of people who were considered the "out" crowd. One of the "uncool" things they did was go to church. So, at first, I went faithfully to Mass too.

I'm not sure how it happened, but I suddenly found myself accepted by the "in" group at school. It was an irresistible temptation, because at high school, I failed to make it into the "in" group — to tell the truth, I was considered a real poop in high school — but here, for the first time, I was accepted by people who, from my 17-year-old vantage point, seemed to have it all together.

Of course, there were rules of membership, none of them written down or even spoken of, but rigid and binding nonetheless. Rule one was, you didn't hang around with "out" people. You also didn't go to church. After a few arguments with my new friends, I stopped going. I felt that I should be attending Mass, but my feelings were based on a sense of duty, not on any awareness of a personal connection with God. I knew my mother would be really upset if I didn't go.

So I didn't tell her.

****

One of the "in" crowd became a special friend of mine, a girl named Joan. We had a lot in common, including a desire to follow our nurses' training with training to be midwives. I'm not sure what prompted that — perhaps it was because we were ardent, if not very thoughtful, feminists at that time, and being a midwife seemed a very modern, progressive, feminist thing to do.

Midwifery training was not available in the United States, so Joan and I decided to go farther from home than I had ever imagined. We applied for midwifery studies in England, the centre for those kind of studies, and we were accepted. Besides, as I mentioned before, I had ulterior motives for a trek across the Atlantic, a dream that was squashed by a Dear Anne letter only two weeks after we arrived.

My plans for England fell through on every count. I did not catch the guy I chased all those thousands of miles, and I did not complete training in midwifery. But my life was changed, dramatically and unalterably, in those months across the ocean.

It took almost a year from the time Joan and I applied to go to work and study in England, before everything was approved. So we worked as nurses in the U.S., waiting for all the details to fall into place. But finally, everything was set for the trip.

When we finally got to England, we decided it would be a good idea, before actually starting the course, to work in a regular English hospital, to learn what nursing and medical care were like there, and to gain some familiarity with British hospital techniques, which can be quite different from America. We got jobs at the Churchill Hospital in Oxford, which was built during the Second World War. For us, it sometimes felt as though the war had never ended — we were living in Nissen huts built behind the hospital.

I worked in the neurology division — that had been my speciality, although it related not at all to midwifery — and Joan, who wanted more experience in gynaecology, worked on that ward, probably a more appropriate assignment, considering our ultimate goal.

While she was working on her ward, Joan met a young orderly who was doing that job to pay his way through Cambridge university. They spent a lot of time talking to each other, but neither Joan nor I realized that his real interest was in her friend — me! I guess he liked me, although I'm not sure why, because he didn't know me very well.

Somehow David found out that September 8 is my birthday. On September 8, as I was working on the neurology ward, I began to receive silly little birthday presents. One after another, David kept giving me these very inexpensive gifts, all day. One, I remember, was a pack of Smarties. We're not talking diamonds and furs, here, but I really thought it was sweet of him.

I guess diamonds and furs were not necessary, because I immediately accepted when he asked me out on a date. By the time I left England, six months later, we were engaged — although I wasn't completely convinced this was a good idea. Despite the changes in me through nursing school and my experiences in England, I was still very conservative, and David seemed to me to be something of a hippie — he was a student, pursuing studies in languages, something that to my practical, nursing mind seemed to be taking him nowhere in terms of a career.

I thought that returning home would give me a clearer perspective on the relationship. It might have, except David continued his unique methods of courtship. I still don't know where he got the money to do it, but three times that year, as I was walking down the street in Con-

20

cord, David would suddenly appear. He'd flown over from England, just to see me.

He left school, and on February 2, 1974, we were married. And he decided to become a police officer in England for a very practical reason — bobbies in Britain might not have been highly paid, but they were given a house to live in. David became a cop to put a roof over our heads. He joined the police force in Bicester, and I got a job with the Radcliffe Infirmary in Oxford.

David's original motive for becoming a police officer may not have been exceedingly noble, but as soon as he donned the high Bobby's hat, he knew that he had found a career he would enjoy. I was married to a man who quickly came to love his job as a cop.

Working at the Churchill Hospital led me to David Packer. That was the good news. But working there also gave me my first real exposure to one of the worst horrors in the world. It was at that English institution for healing that David and I first encountered the appalling reality of abortion.

Doctors and nurses who had vowed their commitment to the preservation of life were killing babies. Dozens of babies were being aborted, every day.

Chapter Three

Encounter With Death

I had encountered abortion before, although never at the stark level of reality that hit me at Churchill hospital. Being raised as a Roman Catholic, I always said that I was against abortion. That was as natural to me as praying the Rosary. Abortion was wrong.

At least, that's what I said. In reality, I didn't care. I might have said that I cared, but I didn't care enough to do anything at all about the ongoing destruction of human life. It didn't touch me, and I didn't worry about it.

You can't really call that "caring", although I'm afraid it represents the true feelings of an awful lot of people who say they care about the issue, and who would insist that they are opposed to abortion. If you care, what are you doing about it?

The truth about me is even worse than just "not caring". In reality, I participated, in a kind of passive way, in procuring an abortion. When I was in training to be a nurse, one of my friends became pregnant, and decided to get rid of the baby. She asked me — actually, she pleaded with me — to accompany her to the abortion clinic. I agreed.

Oh, I knew what was happening was wrong. There was no doubt in my mind about that. I had even tried to talk her out of having the abortion. But when my arguments didn't change her mind, I succumbed. I rationalized the whole thing.

I remember thinking this way: "She's my friend, she's going to do it anyway, and she's told me she has no one else to accompany her. She told me she was terribly afraid, afraid of the abortion and also afraid that her mother might find out what had happened."

So, I went along, sat in the waiting room while they did the abortion, and took her home.

It was only later that I found out that she had had several previous abortions, and had asked me to go with her because she was too embarrassed to ask a couple of other close friends who had accompanied her on her former trips to the abortion clinic. Her series of abortions was rapidly using up her supply of sympathetic friends.

But the point is, I played a role in obtaining an abortion, I rationalized my involvement, and then I forgot about it. It took a terrible experience in England to really bring the reality, the horror of the destruction of babies home to me. And even then, my response had nothing to do with helping to save the lives of one of the world's most endangered species — babies.

****

We hadn't been at the hospital in England for very long before it became apparent to me that a lot of their work there involved doing abortions. They did regular D and C abortions in the operating theatre, but there was also a large, experimental programme which involved an enormous number of abortions.

There was one doctor at the hospital, who was also a professor of medicine, who was doing experiments using prostaglandin and related drugs. Prostaglandin is a naturally-occurring hormone which in the female body seems to play a role of some sort in starting labor. Medical experts still aren't completely sure what causes a pregnant woman to go into labor, but they believe this hormone is involved in some way.

As I understand it, this doctor was doing research on using prostaglandin to induce natural labour to help women who were unable to go into labour on their own. Of course, they couldn't experiment on women who wanted to keep their babies — that would have been too dangerous for the "wanted" children — so the subjects of the research were women who were very far along in their pregnancies, but who wanted to end their pregnancies through abortion.

Almost all of the women who were the subjects of the experimentation had been refused more conventional abortions because they were too far into their pregnancies. Some were very close to their delivery date. So the doctor had women coming from all over the country, and he would administer the hormone or drug to them.

Many were so advanced in pregnancy that the babies would be born alive, and then left to die. But some of the drugs he was experimenting with were so strong, or the dosages were so big, that some of the babies were born dead, very clearly having gone through agony in death.

I knew about this because Joan told me. Since she was working in gynaecology, she knew exactly what was taking place. One of her complaints was that because the work was so emotionally stressful, many of the staff had refused to work with the abortion experiments, and she was left with a very unfair workload.

I think she was also uncomfortable with the experiments going on, but when she talked about it to other members of the medical staff, they told her she was crazy. There was no problem. Nothing immoral or unethical was going on, they said. In fact these women were getting exactly what they wanted, and everybody should be happy about it.

Nobody considered for a minute what the smaller human beings involved would have wanted.

And I'm not so sure that the women who had the abortions really got what they wanted, either. Joan told me that one of the toughest parts of her job was dealing with women who must have thought they were getting rid of some excess tissue, or something, and instead discovered that a well-developed baby had just been killed.

I don't really know what they expected, because by that time the baby would have been moving around inside them, but when they realized what had really happened, many of them were terribly, utterly upset.

So, in addition to having extra-duty nursing responsibilities in a very unpleasant situation, Joan also found herself having to comfort hysterical, emotionally upset women on many occasions. She began to have terrible nightmares. We were still sharing accommodations, and often I would rouse from my sleep to find her awake in the night, sweating, crying and very, very upset.

I wasn't working on that floor. But I was employed by the same hospital, I knew what was happening, a floor or two away from me. I knew that part of my paycheque was made possible through the deliberate killing of babies.

Since then, I've asked David, "Why weren't we upset? Why didn't we do anything right then?" I knew the terrible things that were taking place right there in the hospital I was working in, and so did he. One of his friends who was also an orderly had the unnerving experience of carrying bags of garbage to the incinerator, and discovering to his shock that the bag was moving.

One of the late-term, aborted babies must have been in that garbage bag, still alive. But trying to do anything about it would have caused a terrible fuss, and David's co-worker simply disposed of the bag with all of the others.

Both David and I were aware of all of this. And we did nothing.

David has a simple explanation for our terrible failure to do what we both knew, even then, was the right thing to do. He says, "We were too selfish, we were too interested in ourselves. We didn't care about anybody or anything else."

I have to admit, he's right.

The horror came even closer to me one night when I came off shift and went to find Joan. We officially finished shift at the same time, but because she was often working alone on that terrible duty, a lot of the time she was late getting off.

So I went down to her ward to find her. I had never been on that ward before, and I remember being surprised that it was very modern. The rest of the hospital matched the Nissen huts out back — it was all World War II vintage, and looked it. But Joan's ward had all the latest in hospital design and equipment. Even then, it struck me, how ironic it was that the wards which existed to preserve life were outmoded, while the place where doctors were killing people, not saving them, was so up-to-date.

But I didn't let myself think about that for very long.

There were a lot of hallways in that section of the hospital, and I couldn't find Joan right away. I was wandering around rather aimlessly, looking for my friend in this hospital maze.

I finally ended up in front of the white door of the sluice room. The sluice room is rather like a combination bathroom and dishwashing room. It contains the bedpan washer, and has a big sink where all sorts of other utensils end up. It's also a handy place to put the garbage before the orderlies haul it away.

I wondered if Joan might be inside, so I walked in. I was confronted with the most horrific sight I had ever seen in my life.

There were tiny bodies all over the place. There must have been at least nine or ten bodies of babies who had been aborted that day. There were so many, and many of the babies looked as though they were fully developed.

I stopped, cold. I found myself slowly backing out of the room, unable to tear my eyes away from the horror that was lying on the counters, in the sink, on the floor. I clearly remember that my mouth dropped open, and I couldn't close it again. The hair was standing up on the back of my neck. I had that knot in the pit of my stomach that I remembered from being scared to death when I was a kid.

All I wanted to do was run, to get away, anywhere. It was like living out the most terrifying nightmare. And, just like it happens in bad dreams sometimes, I could only move in slow motion. I just wanted to take off, but I could barely move.

I slowly backed out the doorway, my eyes riveted to the sight of the bodies of babies. There was no possible doubt about what these were. Earlier that day, these had been living human beings, growing and thriving inside the wombs of their mothers. Now, they were corpses, dead human beings. The hospital in which I was working was killing babies. There was no other way to look at it.

I finally got out of the sluice room — it seemed to take forever — and I found Joan. She told me that what I had seen wasn't at all exceptional; this was the normal amount of "refuse" produced in a day's activities on her ward. Ten or more babies a day.

I wish I could tell you that it was that experience that turned me around, that forced me to become involved in the fight to save the lives of unborn children. I wish I could write that, that night, David and I sat down and decided to become involved, to do whatever we could to stop this atrocity.   But that would be a lie.

Instead, I ran away. I said, in the last chapter, that I came back to America after six months to get a bit of thinking space about my relationship with David. But when I look deep inside, I think I really started to leave right there, that night, as I backed out of the sluice room.

Somewhere inside, that episode had planted a seed of horror in me. And, while I wasn't willing to actively get involved in the issue, I began to want to get as far away from it as possible.

Despite all of my denial, despite my rationalizing discussions with Joan, I know that I realized, deep in my inner self, that something horrible was going on. I think Joan actually knew it too, because at just about the same time, we realized that we did not want to become midwives after all.

Without ever asking about it, I think we were both afraid — especially, I was, because I wasn't having the day to day contact with abortions that Joan did — that we would have to become involved in abortions as part of midwifery studies. I don't know if that would have happened, but it became a real concern for me. I knew the teaching hospital that had accepted our applications did abortions, and I couldn't imagine we would have been exempted from that element of nursing duties. I wasn't aware that the Abortion Act for England, Scotland and Wales had always had a conscience clause, which allowed nurses to opt out of abortion-related duties if they were opposed to abortion. Northern Ireland does not have legal abortions.

Canadian nurses have no such choice — there is no "conscience clause" in Canada.

As David found out, more than ten years later, conscience and morality seem to be unacceptable reasons for refusing duty.

As well, our families were eager for us to return to the United States. That was enough extra incentive for us to pack in our plans, pack our bags, and head home. I could always explain I was coming home to be near my folks, but the truth was, I was running away from a horror I didn't want anything to do with.

I'm ashamed to admit it, but just getting away from it seemed to be enough. I didn't feel any need to actively oppose abortion. I was one of that preposterous group of people who say,

"Well, I wouldn't have an abortion, but I won't impose my morality on other people." We're facing an issue of life and death here, a situation where thousands of human beings are being killed, but I didn't want to suggest that it might be wrong to do that.

Ridiculous.

So, I ran away.

****

David was doing the same thing, in England. He didn't even leave his job as an orderly for a while. He ran away just by ignoring the reality of what was going on.

Even though he did not have my Roman Catholic heritage stirring inside, insisting in a quiet voice of conscience that what was taking place was wrong, he also said he believed abortion was evil.

But he was no more involved than I was. If he didn't bother people who were having or giving abortions, they wouldn't bother him. I suspect that, after his co-worker told him about the garbage bag that moved, David simply didn't look too closely at the bags he carried to be disposed of in the incinerator.

We were both like an awful — and I use that word on purpose — an awful lot of people around today. Most people really don't want to be touched by abortion, so they pretend it doesn't exist, or they don't allow themselves to think about or admit to what is really going on.

I understand what that's like. I was able to walk out of a room containing the bodies of fully-developed, recently-killed babies, and all I did was move to another country. If I wasn't near what was going on, it wouldn't affect me. I cared not at all for the effect on the victims of this mass genocide.

It reminds me of a large number of politicians and religious leaders in Canada and the United States today. It's hard to find a political candidate who will say he or she is in favor of abortion. They all seem to say, "I'm personally opposed to abortion, but I don't want to impose my morality on other people."

It's about time that we realized that people who say that kind of thing are really in support of wide-open abortion, however they phrase their euphemistic statements. When we read of a woman being raped in front of a crowd of on-lookers who refuse to help, we are appalled. No one would listen for a moment to someone who said, "I didn't try to stop it because, while I'm personally opposed to rape, I didn't want to impose my morality on the rapist."

And if someone provided money to help the rapist pay for a taxi in order to escape, he or she would be charged as an accessory to a crime, after the fact.

Has it occurred to you that many of your tax dollars are going to help abortionists do their thing? Many of us are accessories before and after the fact, even if we haven't had an abortion, or actively encouraged someone to do so.

In England, David and I were accessories. Finally, I ran away, and he ignored the whole thing. As soon as he could quit his job — when I returned to England to marry him — he did. We protected our own sensibilities; but to that point, we did nothing to protect babies who were being killed. David is right — we were both incredibly selfish, eagerly covering our eyes and ears so we wouldn't be bothered by a gigantic evil taking place all around us.

For both of us, it took something much more immediate to spur us to action in opposition to abortion. I really began to be aware of the true value of children when I was pregnant with our first child, Elizabeth.

But before Elizabeth was born, another very difficult crisis brought me face to face with the most significant change I have ever known in my life.

Chapter Four

A New Beginning

My year back in the U.S. left me convinced that I really did want to marry this unique linguistics expert and hospital orderly who thought a package of Smarties was an ideal birthday present. He'd certainly proven his love and devotion, and he had six used transatlantic airline tickets to show for it.

On February 2, 1974, we were married. David became a cop, and thus got the house that came with the uniform, and we began to settle into married life.

After a year apart, David and I were back together. We were married, had a home, and both of us were working in the careers we had chosen. In the second year of marriage, I became pregnant with Elizabeth, who is now eleven. We should have been very happy.

But we were not. Like many newly-married couples, David and I had our ups and downs settling into our marriage. By the time Elizabeth was conceived, our marriage was in trouble, very serious trouble. Both of us were running away from the other, angry that our partner was not there for us, but unwilling to be there for our partner. I would have to admit that we were very near the end of life together.

And I was pregnant. I love being pregnant — I guess the fact that we have five kids is pretty good evidence of that. I love the awareness of a new life, growing right inside me.

But I've often said that I wouldn't even decide to change the curtains in the house when I'm carrying a baby, especially during the first three months. For me anyway, it seems that all my emotional strength is focused on growing the new life inside me.

There couldn't have been a worse time for a crisis in our marriage to occur. (There also couldn't be a worse time for a woman to decide if she's going to have an abortion. There's every chance her thinking will be emotionally clouded and confused, especially in those early months of carrying a child.)

Surprisingly, I actually did a smart thing, with a little bit of help from my mother. Living in England, I always missed my family, a lot. It was my habit to come home about once a year to visit my folks. I decided at the critical point between David and I to make a trip home It wasn't a trial separation, although I knew that splitting up might be right around the corner. I just was able to find a bit of space, coming home to Mom.

I found a lot more than that.

I flew home to New Hampshire, pregnant, scared, and wanting to hide. The last thing I wanted to hear from my mother was, "I'm attending a prayer group, and since you told me about the problems between you and David, we've been praying for you. Would you be willing to come with me to the group?"

But that's exactly what she said, as soon as I arrived home.

Everything in me cried, "No!" The last thing I wanted was to sit in a room with a bunch of people — all of whom apparently, already knew about my personal problems — staring at me. Besides, going to a "prayer meeting" had a ring to it that was very foreign, coming from my conservative, Catholic mother.

But mother-daughter relationships being what they are, it's not too surprising that I went anyway. I agreed reluctantly, I sat poised on the very edge of my chair — not an easy accomplishment, when you're pregnant — but I went.

A few hours later, I returned to my parents' house utterly, completely changed.

As I wrote earlier, I had fallen far away from being a practising Christian. So, for a number of reasons, I felt a little guilty as I walked into that prayer group with my mother. I was also torn between paranoia (who knows what about me?) and some sense of gratitude that these people had cared enough to pray for me, even though I was living thousands of miles away.

I discovered that this prayer group was part of a new movement in the Roman Catholic Church — the charismatic renewal. Charismatics are Christians who believe the church (not just the Catholic church, but almost every brand of Christian faith) has ignored or missed the work of the third person of the Trinity, the Holy Spirit. So, for that matter, had I — I knew nothing at all about the present-day work of the Spirit of God.

The Bible talks a lot about the work and the gifts of the Holy Spirit. In the early church, miracles were a frequent occurrence. People were healed, there were messages of prophecy, teachers and preachers were divinely inspired, and believers spoke in languages they had never learned (called speaking in tongues), both to communicate the message of Jesus to foreigners, and simply to praise God.

Many of these things have been largely missing from the church for centuries. But, in the past twenty years or so, there has been a miraculous resurgence of the work of the Holy Spirit. Of course, I knew nothing about that, at all. This was all news to me.

What I did discover was, when these people at the prayer group asked if they could pray for me, they didn't mean that they would sit quietly and pray silently in their places. They also didn't mean they would read some prayer from a book of prayers.

Those believing people gathered around me, laid their hands on me, and began to pray. They prayed as though they really knew God, and genuinely expected Him to do something. They asked God to baptize me in His Holy Spirit (a phrase from the Bible that means the Spirit of God fills your whole being).

And God heard their prayers, and answered them. It was one of the greatest moments in my life. They asked God to fill me, and boy, did He ever!

I fell apart. I sobbed, and I wept, and I felt, for the first time in a very long time, that God loved me. I knew then that He had always loved me and had always been there with me.

I know that when I write about being filled with the Holy Spirit, it may sound strange — but after it has happened to you, you realize that it is a perfect description of what God does at that moment. I had always had a sense that God was watching my life, caring about my life. Now, I strongly felt that God was right inside my life.

I realized, suddenly, that Jesus was the answer to the guilt I carried. It was true that I could never be good enough for God, but Jesus, God's gift to me and to all of humanity, is the living evidence that God loves me anyway.

That night, as I finally realized that God loved me, I could no longer refuse Him.

How can you reject someone who loves you that much? It may sound like a cliche, but it's true: that was the beginning of a whole new life, for me. I walked out of that prayer meeting realizing that a phrase that is constantly mocked and ridiculed these days is actually wonderfully true. I felt "born again."

It may sound strange, but two things happened at the same time: I realized that I was loved by God, and therefore that I was special; and I also realized how terrible a wife I had been. It was a little like a really serious "Good news/ bad news" joke — although I soon realized that it all could be "good news."

I must have shocked poor David, very badly. There's nothing more surprising than being geared up for a punch, and receiving a kiss, instead. I returned to England, and I'm sure he thought we were heading for the final showdown. He must have been waiting for the third degree: "What horrible things were you doing while I was away?" and a lot more of the same.

What he heard instead was, "I'm so sorry. I know that I have really hurt this marriage, and that I've also hurt you. Please forgive me."

I suppose it took him a few minutes to get things straightened around in his head. He'd been expecting an attack; instead, he got an apology. I was sincere, too — I knew beyond doubt that I had contributed my share to our problems.

When David realized that I meant what I was saying, he quickly developed a whole new viewpoint on marriage. Until then, our miserable marriage had been something he wanted to escape. Suddenly, it was very much something worth keeping. I heard my husband say, "I'm sorry, too. I know I've hurt you very much. I will never do anything like that again. Will you forgive me, too?"

We weren't instantly OK, completely free of anger or pain at that moment. But just as the baptism of the Holy Spirit was the beginning of a new life for me, those expressions of forgiveness were the beginning of a whole new marriage, a relationship that has been pretty darn wonderful ever since. We had hurt each other terribly, but it wasn't long before we both were honestly able to say that those things were behind us, and that the good that was growing rapidly had replaced the bad.

It took about six months before we had really worked through everything — all the hurt, all the confession, all the genuine forgiveness. But by the time Elizabeth was born, she arrived to a happy home with a united mom and dad.

I thank God for David Packer — an emotion I would never have felt before that November prayer meeting.

****

There was one other direct result from my encounter with Jesus. It had turned me around, and put our marriage on a solid foundation for the first time. It also started to change my thinking, and my actions, concerning abortion.

I've found that when you have a real relationship with God, it goes hand-in-hand with being pro-life. Being in the pro-life movement has enhanced my religious life tremendously, incredibly.

I've discovered, in talking to other people, that this is true for a lot of them as well. They've found that they cannot live lives close to God without strongly sensing His displeasure with the death of unborn children. I know that abortion is an abomination to God, that He hates what is going on.

I could not begin my new life with Him without, very soon, realizing that I could no longer avoid responding to the horrors that I had seen and heard about.

I've already said that David is a quiet man. I love to talk; he loves to listen. It's not a bad combination, actually. He's less obviously emotional than I am, and slower to throw himself, holus-bolus into some new idea or project.

It was that way with faith in Christ, and with the pro-life movement. At first, I think I was afraid that David was not with me in these areas. But I soon realized that, in his own quiet way, my husband was growing in faith in God, and that he, too, was deeply concerned about the evil of abortion. He has since said that his concern about abortion really sprang from those experiences at Churchill hospital — the babies in the sluice room, and in the garbage bag.

We had come close to separation before. I'm sure that God was not going to allow differences of opinion to drive us apart, again. We were growing together.

It's very important to remember that my growth with God coincided exactly with Elizabeth's growth inside me. That combination of experiences focused me on the wonder of birth, and the horrible alternative of abortion, like nothing else ever could have.

When I first learned that I was pregnant, I couldn't believe it. I was very fortunate — I felt well, all the time. I was never sick. That first pregnancy was just a dream.

I'll never forget the constant wonder I felt as I started to grow larger around my middle, and then, later, as I felt the baby move inside me. I treasured every kick, every hiccup of that child. Those are amazing experiences, something that someone who has never carried a child could never understand.

I'm sure that even David would not fully understand, although he was excited and supportive throughout the pregnancy. He admitted that seeing another person move around inside me seemed very strange to him, but he was fascinated by the entire process.

When I gave birth to our first daughter, he was right beside me all the way, and I was so moved when I realized that my quiet, unemotional husband was weeping as he watched his daughter being born.

From the very first days that I knew I was pregnant, I felt an incredible bond with my child. I thought about her all the time. She was as real to me as any person I knew. In a way, she was more real, because she was with me all the time, in a sense a very real part of me.

I would often sit and rub my stomach and think about the baby. I spent hours talking to her, and I listened to my favorite music, hoping that the baby would be soothed as I was.

I love "The Winter" from Vivaldi's Four Seasons, and I've sat in front of the stereo speakers with the music blasting away, sharing it with my yet-to-be-born baby.

These things are not only true with Elizabeth. I've shared these experiences with each of my five children, long before I knew what sex they would be, or what their names might be.

Being pregnant is not easy. Not all of my pregnancies have been the dream that the first one was — maybe God realized that I had gone through enough stress in my relationship with David, and blessed me with an easy nine months.

I've also suffered miscarriages, and those have been among the most heartbreaking experiences of our marriage.

But although pregnancy is not always easy, it's always wonderful. It's difficult at times, carrying all that weight. You are often sick, usually tired, and there are those terrific side effects, like hemmorhoids or varicose veins. But those are unimportant side issues.

The reality is, you're bringing a baby into the world. God has blessed you with a child. That's just great.

As I grew larger with Elizabeth inside me, I did everything I could to educate myself about childbirth and the development of the baby in the womb. I already knew a fair amount from my nursing training, but I bought all of the books, like "A Child Is Born," I read everything I could get my hands on, and I went to the pre-natal classes. David came with me to the classes when he could.

In the middle of the year, our first daughter was born.

****

But as I said, something else had already come to life, as well. As I studied and learned about the baby that was growing inside me, I had obviously also been learning about babies in general. As I looked at pictures of children in the womb, I

41

could no longer escape the reality of what abortion really was.

I began to realize how stupid my ideas had been. I became aware that my argument about not imposing my morality on others completely ignored the truth, that we weren't talking about women's rights concerning their own bodies. We were talking about the deaths — to put it straight, the murder — of babies who were just as real, just as much human beings, as the baby I was carrying in my womb. Hundreds, thousands of Elizabeths were being killed and dumped into garbage bags. I was overcome at times with the horror of it.

I knew without any question at all that I would never have an abortion. I could not kill my child. And if my child is a person, then everybody else's children are people, too. I realized, to my shame, that believing that it would be OK for someone else to kill their child, because they owned it, was absolutely, without doubt, the stupidest thing I had ever thought in my life.

Yet almost every argument in support of abortion uses the "ownership" idea, even if they don't put it in those words. Women have the right to control their own bodies, because they own them. Therefore they have the right to have an abortion. That implies two things that are plainly ridiculous — that the growing baby is simply a part of its mother's body; and that the mother owns the baby.

If I were walking down the street and I saw somebody beating up a baby, I wouldn't quibble about ownership. That baby is a human being, and no one has a right to damage or kill another human being.

No one owns anyone — that sort of thing was abolished 100 years ago or more, and thank God that it was.

When you become a mother, when you have a baby, then somehow all the world's children are your children, too. As a mother, in some mystical way, all children become important to you. And that includes the children who are not yet born.

I had always liked children. I earned money by babysitting when I was in school, and I enjoyed that job.

But being a mother has taken me far beyond "liking kids." It's not that I always think my kids are absolutely wonderful — sometimes they can be a real pain — but most of the time motherhood is the highlight of my life. Being a mother fulfills something in me. Something came to life in Anne Packer when my children were born.

That's an extra source of sadness to me, about abortion. Not only is a baby being killed, but something important in a mother is dying too. You cannot kill your baby without searing some very deep-seated emotional scars on your soul.

****

While I was pregnant, there were nights when I simply could not sleep because of the horror of what I had learned about abortion. I would lie in bed with my hand on my stomach, torn between the wonder of the child that was growing in me, and the horrendous evil of the deaths of babies like those I had seen in that hospital sluice room.

I don't know if there was a specific moment when I really began to get angry about abortion, but I know that as Elizabeth grew in me, and I grew in my love for God and for David, a genuine, righteous anger was also growing in me.

My first reaction was absolute frustration. I had hidden from the truth for so long, that when I finally acknowledged what was really going on, I felt completely helpless. I just wanted to tear my hair out, I was so frustrated and angry.

But I did what anyone should do, as they become aware of this catastrophe that is destroying our children. I began to read. Most of what I read made me even more angry, but I knew that I needed the facts before I did anything else. Anything concerning abortion that I could get my hands on, I read.

I didn't just read quietly to myself. I also read to David. And since reading is one of the passions of his life, he read at least as much as I did.

We came to care, more and more, for those unborn babies who would never have the chance for life that we were giving to Elizabeth. We also came to care — and this is something many pro-abortion people fail to understand — for the women who were the victims of the abortion fad. Women were blindly walking into an act that would hurt them for the rest of their lives. In the name of freedom, women were being invited into a lifelong emotional bondage.

The first real anti-abortion action I took was to write a letter to a newspaper in England. When I had read enough to be confident that I had the facts, I wrote a letter to the editor. We didn't join any organized, pro-life groups in England, but I began to write letters, and to take notice of the constant debate that letters on the subject seemed to cause.

From the responses to my letters, and to others in the papers,I became more aware of how controversial a topic this was. I had my first experiences of having my opinions attacked by people writing in response to the letters. That's something anybody involved in pro-life work has to get used to, really quickly. This is an emotionally-charged issue, one in which two sides feel very strongly. When you tell a pro-abortion person that what they are doing is murder, it shouldn't be too surprising if you are attacked in return.

But I cannot believe that taking some criticism from time to time is too high a price to pay to prevent the killing of innocent, unborn children. Obviously, a baby is worth so much more than that.

Writing letters isn't enough. It's not all we must do to fight the evil of abortion. But for me, it was a start. For a conservative, non-confrontational girl from New Hampshire, it was the first move in a long battle, a war in which we're now on the front lines.

When we came to Canada from England, we continued to play our part in the battle for the lives of our children; a fight that has now taken my husband before a police tribunal, that has placed my shy spouse on the front pages of many newspapers, and will probably mean the end of his career.

When my first letters to the English newspapers were attacked by pro-abortion writers, I was not sorry I had written. I'm not sorry now. I'm only sorry that we didn't do more, sooner. We can't go back. But we can go on, with as much energy and determination as this life and death challenge demands of us.

Chapter Five

A Cop in Canada

Coming to Canada was a big decision for David and me. There were several factors involved in making that choice: I wanted to be closer to my family, and the British economy was struggling. So, for that matter, was our personal Packer economy.

I can't help but believe, now, that the real reason we came, although we didn't know it then, was that God wanted us here; that David got his job with the Metropolitan Toronto Police Department for a reason. We probably haven't learned all of that reason yet. Maybe we never will.

******

After Elizabeth was born, we found it very hard to make ends meet. I quit working and, although our house was provided for us, David's salary was too low for comfort. Things were tight. As well, I missed my family, and we decided it was the right time to make a major move. (Ironically, almost immediately after we left, the police officers in David's former department were given a large pay increase).

We chose Canada because it seemed to be a good compromise for an Englishman and an American woman. Coming to Canada would make it easier for David to find a job, but I would be only a few hours — instead of a whole ocean — away from my family.

David applied for a post with the Metropolitan Toronto Police Department, and was notified that he had been accepted. That prompted us to sell all our possessions, pack the essentials of life, and we got ready to move.

But just before we were about to leave England, we received a telegram from the Toronto police department. There had been some mistake, it said. Quotas at the department were full, and there wasn't a job for David after all.

By that time, there also wasn't a job for him in England, and we were without a house, furniture, or any of the basic necessities of life.

We decided to come anyway, but we arrived in Canada with very little optimism to declare at Customs. However, the department found a job for David as a "Green Hornet" — a bylaw enforcement officer — which he kept until an opening came up at the police college, six months later. Like any police officer coming to Ontario from another country, David was required to undergo additional training before he could actually become a functioning police officer. Laws and regulations vary considerably from country to country.

David was happy to be back in uniform, but he found police work in Canada to be very different from that in England. He discovered that the uniformed officers are under a lot of pressure, a good deal of it not caused as much by the job, as by their superior officers. The senior officers are often not very kind or very understanding toward their men. To tell the truth, the Metro police department is unlikely to win any awards for employee relations.

That kind of pressure can build up, when the Toronto constables are also facing the significant stress of having to deal, on the job, with everyone from criminals to lawyers to all kinds of pressure groups.

None the less, David is the sort of man who can find good in almost any situation. A lot of that good comes from inside him — he's usually able to let the pressure run off his back, and just get on with his job.

And, usually, he really likes the job itself. David is a wonderful, community-conscious police officer.

He occasionally was given the opportunity to use his abilities with languages. He is very proud that as an officer who has English — and we're really talking "English", here — as his first language, he has served as a translator in both Spanish and French.

And it's ironic. His assignment to the community foot patrol of 14 Division was the change that led to all this trouble, because it is officers on foot patrol who must guard the Morgentaler clinic. But he was really looking forward to another aspect of police work attached to foot patrol, working with the Vietnamese community in Toronto.

Our city is renowned, world-wide, for its large ethnic communities. We have our own Chinatown, a huge Italian section, Greek and Caribbean communities, and parts of the city that are primarily populated by dozens of other ethnic groups. Cultural festivals are a large part of the entertainment life of Toronto. It gives a wonderful, cosmopolitan flavor to the city.

One of the newer sections is the Vietnamese community. And that particular group has severe problems with extortion, as unscrupulous people try to take advantage of their own community. This presents obvious difficulties in policing, when the department is largely English-speaking, without a lot of background concerning the Vietnamese culture.

David was hoping to become attached to the Asian Unit, to help the community solve some of its internal problems. He was teaching himself the Vietnamese language, and was spending many of his off-duty hours in Vietnamese restaurants, familiarizing himself with the language and with the community.

Now, I guess that is all a broken dream. I think the city has lost an awfully good potential member of the Asian Unit.

Pardon my language, but I think it's a bloody shame.

I think that David's police record would bear this out. Since he joined the force he has received 10 commendations for good police work, including "exceptional arrests and investigative follow-up", "excellent police work", and "professionalism" — this latter one, in January of 1987, only a few months before he was charged with insubordination.

But I think one incident says more about his approach to his job than any other.

David and his partner were called to an apartment building where there was a fire in progress. They crawled into the burning apartment on their hands and knees, and rescued a Vietnamese woman.

She was a deaf-mute, but managed to get her message across to David and the other officer by her own form of sign language. She held her arms together and rocked — her baby was still in the apartment!

David crawled back into the burning apartment, and found the baby. When he emerged from the smoke, he discovered that the infant had stopped breathing. David performed CPR (cardio-pulmonary resuscitation) and the child recovered. The baby is fine today.

David was awarded a commendation for bravery for his actions in saving the child. But it is his response to that incident that tells me even more about my husband than does his bravery.

He's so quiet, and unassuming. That night, when he returned home from his shift, he told me nothing about the fire, or his action in saving the child. I remember that night, only because he smelled strongly of smoke (neither of us uses tobacco), but I only assumed that he must have shared the squad car with a new partner who smoked heavily. I didn't ask, and he didn't say a word.

I finally learned the whole story about six months later, and then only after he found out that he was to receive an award and a plaque, from the department, for his efforts.

To top the whole incident off, David was very embarrassed about the award. He felt he was simply doing his job as a police officer, and that he did not deserve special attention. He argued that other cops had performed equally brave deeds, which had never been acknowledged. In fact, he decided not to attend the awards ceremony.

That left Toronto police chief Jack Marks, or one of his representatives, standing alone, holding an award with no one to present it to. I guess the powers that be were somewhat embarrassed, themselves — David was given the award later, but he was also disciplined for not showing up!

But that's what my husband is like. He does his job well and he likes to stay out of the limelight. And that's why his decision to refuse the order to do duty at the Morgentaler "clinic" was such an enormously brave decision for him — he would do almost anything to avoid the attention he has since received.

******

In England, I had been writing letters to newspapers, in protest against abortion. Once we came to Canada, our interest grew, as did our experience — and, I suppose, our anger. Here, we joined several pro-life groups. We first became members of Toronto Right to Life, and then Campaign Life and Human Life International. Each of these is a fine organization, making important contributions to the fight to save the lives of the children.

As well, we began to attend pro-life events and rallies. I think the first such event was the Mothers' Day March in Toronto, sponsored by Right to Life. We both went, and the demonstrators would march from Queen's Park, the seat of Ontario's government, and proceed down University Avenue, past the hospitals where abortions are being done.

Of course, once the Morgentaler abortuary was opened on Harbord Street, we also marched there. David marched at the abortuary, and he was very open about it; he didn't try to hide, or to get lost in the crowd. He knew several of the police officers who were on duty at the clinic, and he said "Hi" to them as he walked by.

His views on abortion weren't a surprise to anyone. He's also had a pro-life bumper sticker on his car for years. It reads, "Everybody deserves a birthday — Adoption, not abortion."

One of the great ironies of our day is that prospective adoptive parents have to wait for years to adopt a baby, because almost all of the babies who might be available to these loving homes are being killed in abortuaries and hospital operating rooms. Adoption is a wonderful alternative to abortion, but one that is, by and large, ignored today.

The reality that there are adoptive homes awaiting babies makes a complete mockery of the pro-abortion slogan, "Every child a wanted child." These children are wanted, desperately, by parents who are eager and willing to care for them.

Marching in a demonstration like the Mothers' Day March is hard for David, because he really doesn't like crowds. I think that's a result of being raised in a small village. But he believes in the pro-life cause so much that he sets his personal likes and dislikes aside to make a point that has to be made.

One thing he was reluctant to do, was to join me specifically in picketing the Morgentaler abortuary. He would walk past it in a major march, but he didn't see how he could picket it one day when he might be called on to guard it the next.

He obviously felt torn between two loyalties — his allegiance to the protection of human lives that were being ended through abortion, and his allegiance to his paid position as a policeman, an officially-assigned protector of human lives. That was before he decided that guarding the "clinic" was not a legitimate part of his police duties, and he made his courageous decision to refuse to guard an abortuary that was killing babies.

At 12:30 p.m., April 8, 1987, my husband resolved that conflict within himself. He put his career and his reputation on the line, took a giant step past marching in demonstrations,and walked into the office of his superior officer to refuse to guard the Morgentaler "clinic" on the grounds that, because the place was an illegal abortuary, assignment there was not a legal order, and because he could not, in good conscience, be party in any way to the killing of babies that was taking place there.

Our lives had gone through pretty major changes several times before. But never had those changes occurred in a public spotlight, on the front pages of the newspapers, or before a police tribunal. Constable David Packer was ordered to report to the tribunal to face the charge of insubordination.

Chapter Six

"Don't Destroy The Best"
Mother Teresa

The furore and controversy that have raged because of David's request that day often seem almost silly. In one sense, all that happened was that a police officer asked his boss for alternate duty because he couldn't, in good conscience, carry out the original duties assigned to him that afternoon.

If his superiors had simply said, "O.K., for the next four hours, here's where you're assigned instead," none of the subsequent, and highly public, controversy would have happened.

But when I think about that for a while, I realize there was no chance of that nice, simple solution actually happening. That's because my husband, in one small act, was challenging an entire, immoral system. When you think about the number of abortions that have taken place in Canada, and then realize that every one of those acts involves a mother, a father, and some family members and friends, it quickly becomes apparent that the frightening reality is that the majority of Canadians have a vested interest in believing abortion is not wrong.

I cannot help but believe that, deep inside, most of them know that it is, but many people work awfully hard to bury the truth to maintain a surface level of personal peace. The majority of people would rather avoid the necessity of admitting guilt, repenting, and working to somehow make things right.

Canada has headed straight down what that great British writer, Malcolm Muggeridge, has called "The Slippery Slope". Even when the law said abortion outside a hospital was wrong, self-confessed abortionists like Henry Morgentaler were being acquitted by Canadian juries.

Canadian political leaders were turning a blind eye to offences. Police officers were ordered not to charge abortionists, even though the law stated they were committing crimes, several times a day. Instead, those officers were ordered to guard the very abortuary where the illegal activities were taking place, completely unhindered by authorities who have pledged to uphold the law.

And now, the Supreme Court of Canada has struck down existing laws — weak and unenforced though they were — leaving this country with no abortion law at all. The government of Canada has debated the issue at length, but the closest our Parliamentarians have come to enacting a new law is to defeat every motion presented on the subject, whether pro-life or pro-abortion.

This is a nation that is committing social suicide by killing its young; and a nation that does not want to be reminded of that terrible fact.

Unfortunately for those who wish to remain unaware, David Packer is just such a reminder. He was standing before three superior officers and telling them he couldn't carry out an order, because the order involved closing his eyes to criminal and immoral activity.

They charged him with insubordination. Now, David Packer stands before the entire country, his quiet action reminding all of us that immoral and illegal activities are going on, telling us that we are a nation that kills its young.

There was no way the issue was going to quietly disappear. Without ever intending to be a hero or a symbol, my husband has found himself, for a while, at least, at the centre of a storm of controversy that has raged, nation-wide.

****

The charges against David, and the subsequent conclusion of the police tribunal that he was guilty of insubordination, drew national attention. David was criticized severely in many newspapers and through the other media. Occasionally, he was commended in the public press, but that was much more rare.

The positive response we received came from supporters of the pro-life movement. We received many warm letters, urging us to stand strong. Pro-life publications made David's situation a cause celebre.

But as the controversy grew, as my husband was attacked in the press (I'll go into detail about that in the next chapter),accused of insubordination by his own police department, and facing the loss of his career and the income with which he supported his family of five children, one expression of support stood out from all the others.

Before I write about the criticism or the congratulations, and before I tell you about some of the details of the police tribunal itself, I want to share this with you — a letter of support from Mother Teresa of Calcutta.

We were absolutely dumbfounded when we received the hand-written letter from Mother Teresa, mailed from her mission, the Missionaries of Charity in Calcutta, India. If there is anyone in the world who more symbolizes concern for the downtrodden and underprivileged, I can't imagine who it is. Her letter has been a source of inspiration and courage to both David and me from the day we received it until now.

Mother Teresa wrote:

"An open letter to Constable David Packer, and to whom it may concern,

"Just two years ago, Constable David Packer risked his life to rescue a three-month-old child from a burning building, and was decorated by the Police Force Department for his courage.

"I find it very difficult to understand how such a man could accept duty guarding a building in which live babies are killed, by killing, dismembering them in their mother's womb, through abortion.

"I find it difficult to understand the logic by which you would punish a man who is obviously heroic in trying to save life.

"Why he was a hero two years ago, yet today he must be penalized? Why is an abortion 'clinic' not only permitted to exist, but must be guarded in order to go on killing tiny, helpless, voiceless babies in what should be the safest place in the world, the mother's womb? Those who would stop the killing are prevented from doing so.

"I call upon the government and all concerned in making laws: don't destroy the best sentiments of nobility in your beautiful people by allowing heroes like David Packer to suffer for his courage towards the weakest of humankind — the unborn child — gift of God.

"You would not allow your own child to be torn apart to death, because it is more convenient for some, and to enrich those who should be committed to saving life, not destroying it. Such people have to appear before God one day, even if they do not wish to think of it or believe it.

"The child is a gift of God, created by God, to love and be loved. But if a mother kills her own child, her very own child, her own flesh and blood, and such things are protected by law, then why are we surprised at the continued horror stories we read daily in the newspapers, of brutal murders and other atrocities?

"And so, abortion has become the greatest destroyer of peace and love.

"Each child is formed in the image of God, and is destined to be with God for all eternity. Allow the child to live. Do not be afraid of the child — he or she cannot hurt you.

"As I have said so often, no child, born or unborn, has to feel unwanted and unloved. For remember, Jesus has said, 'If you receive a little child in my name, you receive me.' To be able to see them, we need a clean heart. For a clean heart can see God, and if we see God in each other, we will love one another as God loves each one of us.

"Let us remember — works of love are works of peace, and love begins at home, in our own family by praying together. For the fruit of prayer is faith; the fruit of faith is love; the fruit of love is service; the fruit of service is peace.

"God bless you,
"Mother Teresa"

As you will read in the next chapter, much of what was written about David took a very different slant, compared to this wonderful message. He was criticized and maligned. But that one letter, from one of the most saintly people in our world today, had much more impact on us than 100 criticisms by newspaper columnists and commentators.

We were given even greater assurance, through her pointed expression of prayer and support, that we were on the right side.

There are some people in this world you simply trust, without question. Mother Teresa, who has devoted her life to caring for the underprivileged, the homeless, the desperately needy, is certainly one of those people.

Her letter to David was reported in the daily press, quoted in the newspapers for all the country to read.

I guess we should not be too surprised that those in authority, people who would have been in any reception to greet Mother Teresa, should she come to Toronto, were nonetheless content to completely ignore her advice.

But if no one else was listening, we certainly were.

Chapter Seven

Public Criticism and Controversy

As I have stated before, David was not seeking the public spotlight when he asked to be given another assignment on April 8. I think, from what you have read so far in this book, you are starting to understand the kind of man my husband is — quiet, solitary, preferring never to be the centre of attention. He'd run from any such situation, any time he could.

But his decision to refuse the assignment to guard the Morgentaler clinic put him smack in the centre. I'm proud of how he handled all of the attention, and I'm proud of the way he refused to seek after self-serving publicity. He has retained the inherent humility, the simple, unaffected approach to every aspect of life that has always been part of what has endeared him to me.

But he could not avoid the attention of the media. This story, first broken in the **Toronto Sun** by a columnist who uncovered the whole situation — he did not learn about it from David or me, by the way — swept through all the major papers in the country. Because it was based in Toronto, the Metro Toronto papers gave an enormous amount of attention to the story — pictures, articles, columns and editorials abounded.

I have to admit that the story has all the elements guaranteed to keep it on page one, and in the columns, for weeks on end. It involved

Henry Morgentaler, a man who has consistently been in the media spotlight, and in many ways, is a media darling.

It involved a police officer rejecting an order from his superiors, and most media types are delighted with anything that has a chance of making cops look a little dumb. On this one, they couldn't lose — either one cop would look dumb, or his bosses would.

It concerned abortion, attracted the attention of pro-life groups (usually seen as flaky, right-wing nuts by many in the media). The story was sure-fire.

Generally, the newspapers were less than understanding in their attitude toward my husband, at least in their commentary sections. The vast majority of editorials and opinion columns were on the attack.

The Toronto **Globe and Mail,** for example, carried an editorial that said, in part:

"We feel less comfortable with an officer who decides, for reasons of his (or her) conscience, not to protect certain people and properties. If he believes that abortion is murder — and we note that the operators of the Morgentaler clinic have been convicted of no offence — how far does he extend the principle? Would he refuse to protect hospitals where legal abortions are performed? Or the houses of people who work at the clinic? Once police officers start to pick and choose among those people who deserve their protection, who among us can feel safe?

"...An officer who refuses to guard such premises is allowing his personal sympathies with the protesters' cause to interfere with his sworn duty to protect life and property, the fundamental duty of an officer of the law.

"A police force, sensitive to a member's dilemma, might attempt where possible to give him an alternative assignment. But the officer should not expect such treatment as a matter of course; and, when he refuses to serve and protect as ordered, he should be prepared to accept the consequences."

This editorial is typical of much of the comment in the newspapers. There is a lot of sense in it, in some ways, but it is based in apparent misunderstandings, both of David's position and request, and of the situation concerning the abortuary.

There is much emphasis given to the fact that David must be prepared to accept the consequences of his action. Of course he is. He was, from the beginning of all of this. He made his decision to refuse to obey the order to guard Morgentaler's clinic, fully aware of the possible outcome.

On the other hand, he feels the action by the police department — and the official tolerance, especially under the law existing at that time, of the Morgentaler clinic — to be in error. Therefore, he has every right to fight for justice, both for himself, and for unborn children who are victims much more than David will ever be.

The **Globe** suggested that an alternative assignment would be a viable solution. It is interesting that this is exactly what David asked for. However, there has been little or no notice of this fact in the press.

The basic disagreement between David and the media is in the role the police officers play at the Morgentaler clinic. They are not there, first of all, to keep the peace, the primary commitment of police officers. They are there to guard property in which, at that time, admittedly illegal activities were taking place, and people who, at that time, were doing those illegal things.

It was clearly against the law to do abortions at the Harbord Street "clinic." It was freely admitted that abortions were exactly what were being performed there.

That point seems, too often, to be overlooked in the media as they present what the reader is to understand is a reasoned approach to the issue. Like the **Globe and Mail,** too often, they missed the point.

On May 16, the **Toronto Sun** began an editorial this way:

"Constable David Packer is wrong."

The paper continued the article to say:

"Our conclusion has nothing to do with his opposition to abortion, but everything to do with the duty of every police officer.

"His defenders say he only did what killers like Adolf Eichmann should have done: Refused to obey orders.

"The analogy's glib but inept. Packer was not ordered to participate in mass killings of Jews. He was ordered to stand guard outside the Morgentaler Clinic to protect the clinic and its personnel from demonstrators."

This is the kind of reasoning that I simply do not understand. No, let me put that another way — I believe I do understand the "thinking" that lies behind this argument, but I do not understand how rational people can honestly think this way. But as several pro-life writers have pointed out, reason was the first thing to die in this issue.

Abortion is the killing of unborn human beings. There is no evidence to conclusively challenge this position. Babies grow inside the womb, and then are born. There is no change in a baby from the moment before birth to the moment after.

In fact, modern medical technology is keeping premature babies alive at earlier and earlier stages of development. These babies are human beings. Abortion is killing a human being before it escapes the womb, often later in the term than the point at which babies can survive on their own!

That's why the analogy which the **Sun** rejects is entirely appropriate. A concentration camp guard who did not actually kill anyone, but who protected those who did, is still considered to bear responsibility for the atrocities committed there.

How is a police officer who is protecting and guarding an abortuary any different? His assignment is to protect someone who is systematically killing human beings. His assignment is also to control, and if necessary, arrest, people who are trying to save the lives of those babies about to be killed.

As Mother Teresa suggested in her letter, there is something desperately wrong with this situation; somehow, things have become morally inverted.

Judge A.K. Meen, presiding over a case involving pro-life demonstrators charged for activities outside the Morgentaler abortuary, made the following statements:

"The fact remains that human lives were being aborted on the dates in question, that the Defendants knew this was occurring and that they were endeavouring to put a stop to it. That is to say, they were doing whatever they could to stop the loss of human life. And it was not as though those human lives were being taken lawfully, for, in fact, the Clinic was operating outside the law, and such was therefore murder.

"The irony of this entire matter is that, on the one hand we have a clinic performing abortions openly, blatantly and outside the law, yet on the other hand all the while enjoying police protection which enabled them to carry on these activities. The Defendants alleged that having exhausted all other avenues which they perceived to be opened to them to put a stop to the taking of human life on the unlicenced premises of the Morgentaler Clinic, they took the only other step left remaining to them and committed the trespass upon those premises. Put into its simplest form, the dilemma raised by this anomaly might be expressed in the question: 'Can the commission of a very minor offence, trespass to private property, be justified when it is committed in an attempt to prevent the commission of a very much greater offence, namely murder?'"

Clearly, we are not alone in seeing the inconsistency in the official position concerning the aborptuary. So, even if the **Toronto Sun** disagrees with our position, surely the writers can understand that it is rational and consistent. But that was seldom acknowledged.

However, one **Toronto Sun** columnist, who is no longer with the paper, was very supportive. Claire Hoy, who has consistently taken a pro-life stance in his columns, wrote:

"If it were up to me, Packer would get a medal for having the courage of his convictions.

"But since it's up to people who may look to the manual rather than to their heart for guidance, chances are he'll be punished.

"It's an odd view of justice."

In that same column, Hoy wrote:

"Like all cops, Packer swore an oath of office, promising to uphold the law 'without favor or affection, malice or ill will...'

"What that means, in law, is if you're assigned to the Morgentaler clinic, you have to accept the order regardless of personal convictions. The question is, must the police always be that rigid?

"Surely not. If there was reason to suspect Packer was being frivolous or just trying to avoid his duty, or there was a riot in progress at the clinic, that's one thing.

"But when his genuine feelings are obvious, what's the harm in reassigning him?"

The **Sun** also carried a letter to the editor which suggested:

"Const. David Packer has to be policeman of the year."

The newspaper, with its usual insistence on having the last word, replied only:

"Bad idea."

There are others who agree with the writer of that letter to the editor. A rally, sponsored by Choose Life Canada in late January, 1988, gave David an award naming him Toronto's "Hero of the Year" for his decision to refuse to guard Morgentaler's "clinic." While my husband is embarrassed about that kind of attention, I know he would more prefer to be recognized for his commitment to this cause than for anything else he has done in his life.

On January 30, 1988, the day before that rally, the **Sun** again editorialized about David's situation. This came after the tribunal had found him guilty as charged, and David had been ordered to resign within seven days, or be fired. That order remains, but is suspended during David's appeal process.

The **Sun** stated:

"There is no question that Const. Dave Packer was wrong."

Later, the editorial reads, "The argument really has nothing to do with abortion... the issue does have everything to do with the rule of law in this pluralistic society which prides itself on tolerating divergent views.

"That only works when the law is enforced by police sworn to uphold it and apply it without prejudice."

The editorial concluded, "An unrepentant Packer says the time had come to stand and be counted....He can't act this way and remain a cop."

This editorial is a good example of why David may lose in this particular case, but those of us who oppose abortion must keep fighting. To say this case has nothing to do with abortion, is ridiculous. To argue that police officers must unthinkingly do absolutely everything they are asked to do, whatever the circumstances, is to invite the danger of an authoritarian system in which conscience no longer matters.

I'm intrigued by the charge that David is "unrepentant." It's not clear from the editorial what it is he should repent about,but I have to suspect a great many people would be much more comfortable if he would "repent" of his opinions that abortion is wrong, and that what is happening at the Morgentaler "clinic" is wrong.

Maybe they would be satisfied if my husband would simply repent of his poor taste in creating a situation in which people have to think about what is happening in their fair land. I don't believe David has anything to repent of, not at all. I do think there will have to be a lot of repentance before the morality of this country can get back on track.

Some people have suggested that because David acted in the way that he did, he is a good cop, a cop who has a conscience, a cop who cares about right and wrong, not only about staying on the good side of his superior officers. It has been suggested that a police force with no David Packers would be a much poorer force indeed.

Wifely prejudice admitted, I agree.

One of the silliest comments that I saw appeared in the business column written by John McLeod, in the **Sunday Sun.** McLeod wrote, in part:

"Business people in particular should be concerned about the potential ramifications of the case of Metro Police Const. David Packer...

"Should Packer's argument be accepted, will we next see police officers refusing to uphold the ... trespassing law because they disagree with it? Will policemen who agree with the aims of the feminist movement be allowed to turn their backs if a feminist rally turns into a riot? Will a constable be able to refuse to lay yet another charge against furrier Paul Magder because he or she thinks it is a matter of 'conscience' to be able to shop on Sundays?"

I've written, earlier in the book, about people who want to ignore the whole question of abortion. I couldn't find a better example. This columnist has equated the sale of goods on Sunday with the death of babies in an abortion "clinic."

I saw a great deal of that kind of thing in the comments on David's case. It is obvious to me that many people, including some prominent writers, are working very hard to reduce abortion to something trivial which it obviously is not.

As long as we can look anywhere else other than the disposal tray that carries the body of a newly-dead baby, we can avoid our own responsibility for the ongoing death.

I urge everyone to take that one, shocking look, see what is really happening, and realize that David did exactly the right thing in refusing to play any part in one of the greatest horrors taking place in our country.

As the most dramatically overstated comment on the whole question, I would have to nominate the **Toronto Star** columnist who included David's situation in a column headlined:

"Police action has Metro sliding into anarchy."

Anarchy is the complete absence of rule. Again, this shows the fundamental misunderstanding of David's approach to the problem. He did not first refuse an order; first, David asked for an alternate assignment. He did not question the right of superior officers to issue an order; he stated that, in his opinion, one particular order was not a lawful order, and he could not, therefore, obey it.

As I suggested earlier, I have to admit that, when it came to direct reporting of the news as it took place, almost all of the accounts that I read were extremely fair. The straight news reporting seemed accurate, and David's statements, as well as those from other pro-life people involved in the situation, were accurately quoted.

But when it came time for the newspapers and their columnists to express editorial opinions — well, it made it even more clear to me how much of a fight we have to emphasize the importance, and the horror, of the abortion situation in our country.

Newspaper writers, by and large, seemed consistently eager to steer their stories away from abortion, and toward other issues, whether they be the imagined danger of anarchy in the police department, or the equally fanciful threat of cops refusing to charge people open on Sundays because of their own personal moral code.

Very few are willing to face abortion, stark, ugly and evil, head-on. And, when you think about it, what happens to one police constable who may or may not lose his job isn't really very important, compared to all of those babies who die, daily.

That, it seems to me, is the real story. I can't imagine why newspaper reporters and editors are not eager to get into the facts of the abortion story, to learn the real truth about what is going on in the "clinics" and hospitals of this country.

That story has more impact on our nation than a dozen police tribunals.

Chapter Eight

New friends and supporters

While the public media was reporting the news, and, through its columns and on its editorial pages, attacking David's stand, the publications from the pro-life movement were rallying strongly behind him. The pro-life publishers seemed to realize, from the very beginning, that here was a man prepared to do what few of us in the movement have been willing to do — David was putting his livelihood, his career and the financial support of his family right on the line because of his strong, moral stand against abortion.

David is not the only person to suffer because of opposition to abortion, but there are not yet many. Some, especially in the United States, have gone to jail for their beliefs and actions. I believe that before unborn babies are safe in this country, and in the other nations of the world (especially, also, the United States) there will be many more.

******

While the news media were attacking our story from their particular slant, **The Interim,** Canada's national pro-life, pro-family newspaper, was giving consistent and sympathetic coverage to David's case. In the June 1987, issue, the same edition that carried a front-page story about David's refusal to guard the Morgentaler clinic, **The Interim** ran a story headed, "David Packer: a cop with a conscience."

Receiving that kind of newspaper into our home certainly gave us a different feeling than we had as we debated whether it was wise to read the **Sun,** the **Globe** or the **Star** that day!

The article, written by Frank M. Kennedy, was based on an interview with David and me. He carefully explained how the situation we now find ourselves in developed. After reviewing the facts, the story concludes with this paragraph:

"At present, Officer Packer is getting little support from his colleagues, apart from lots of good wishes. David is a brave man — a rare individual these days. His courage to stand up for his convictions, knowing all that he has at stake, makes him a man worthy of all our admiration, respect and support."

As I have said earlier, most of the moral support we received did come from people directly within the pro-life movement. Other groups to which we might have looked for help often did not come through in any numbers or with any significant level of enthusiasm.

David's fellow officers, as suggested in the article I quoted immediately above, were often warmly sympathetic in private, and coolly cautious in public statements. We think that they felt — probably correctly — that any indication of support either for David's position, or for some of the statements he made during the tribunal, could put them right up there next to him, facing charges themselves.

That was enough to engender a lot of caution in David's colleagues.

I was even more surprised that more significant support did not come from the churches, especially the Roman Catholic parishes where David and I have attended. It drove home the desperate reality that many people in churches, even in the officially pro-life Roman Catholic church, do not care about the issue of abortion. They "care" in the way I once did — while they may state their opposition to abortion, they are not making the least effort to make a difference.

And, of course, it can be much worse than that. I'm always appalled when I read of Christian leaders, including some Catholics, who maintain it is possible, even desirable, to be both a Christian and be "pro-choice", a phrase I hate. I consider it to be a dishonest euphemism that means "pro-abortion."

But as I have pointed out before, doing absolutely nothing about the abortion that is an on-going threat to our country is exactly the same as being "pro-choice." And that is where I fear a majority of Christian church members would honestly have to place themselves right now, in this country. If this is not true, where are they? Children who may never be allowed to be born need their help!

We certainly did not hear from, nor see the active support of, a majority of Christians in our community. That's a sad commentary on the state of the church, and it's time it changed. If this book can prompt some Christians to re-think their position, then it has done its job. And if my straight talk about Christian cop-outs can shock anyone into action, then I do not apologize, not at all.

There were, of course, significant exceptions to this generalization, and we are deeply grateful for the spiritual support we received from a number of Christian friends and pro-life supporters.

In the October, 1987 issue of **The Interim,** the paper ran a lengthy commentary by Jesuit missionary Lawrence Abello, of Calcutta. (This was the same issue that reported Mother Teresa's support for David).

Father Abello pulled no punches in drawing an analogy of the sort that made the **Toronto Sun** extremely uncomfortable. I'll quote some of Father Abello's argument:

"Blindly following orders to protect the Morgentaler abortuary is exactly what 399 of the 400 officers at 14 Division in Toronto's West End are doing at the behest of the Attorney General. Likewise, blindly following orders is what the elite, 20,000 strong, Paris police force did at the behest of the legitimate Vichy government, under Marshall Petain.

"Like the officers standing guard at the Morgentaler abortuary, the Paris police were never ordered to kill anyone. Many of them were merely ensuring that 'demonstrators' did not disturb 'peace and order' while hundreds of Jewish children destined for death in concentration camps were hauled away in buses.

"But the 'fetuses' killed at the Morgentaler abortuary are not legally persons! Neither were the 'unmenschen' (non-humans) 'which' were being hauled away in the buses. A society always relegates the victims of a holocaust to the status of non-persons in order to hide the injustice it is perpetrating.

"...Those who criticize David Packer's action may claim that he was not ordered to protect an illegal establishment because, they claim, the

Morgentaler abortuary is in legal limbo until the Supreme Court rules on pending charges. But in ensuring 'peace' for the transfer of Jewish children destined for the death camps, the Paris police were protecting a totally 'legal' activity.

"...So, David Packer, by maintaining 'peace' outside the 'clinic' to render possible the killing of babies inside it, you would indeed be getting blood on your hands by association. In fact, you would be no better than the Paris police during the Second World War whose actions every right-thinking person condemns."

I wouldn't change a line in Father Abello's article. I wish I had room to include it all.

I will only say that positive commentary of that sort helped David and me keep everything in perspective, especially during the down times — and there were some of those, including a crisis I'll write about later in the book, when my most recent pregnancy ended in a miscarriage in the spring of 1988.

******

I said earlier that many church groups seem to be terribly uninvolved in this life-and-death struggle against abortion. But there were wonderful exceptions to that generalization, and we were heartened by expressions of support that were directed to us.

One of the most touching, which was was reported in the **Catholic Register** newspaper, came from the students and staff at Pope John Paul II Secondary School, in Scarborough, in east Toronto. The students at that school collected a petition bearing the signatures of more than 500 students and teachers, and presented it to the Metro Toronto Police.

The petition called for all charges against David to be dropped, and asked that he be reinstated to his previous status on the force.

That was not the only petition or demonstration of support that we encountered. I was able to present a petition signed by 57,000 supporters to the police department.

That particular petition, initiated by Mrs. Gerarda Savoie, a great new friend of ours, charged that David had been denied his "conscientious right to object to protecting a building where unborn babies are being killed daily in complete violation of criminal law."

I wanted to present the petition to Police Chief Jack Marks. Not too surprisingly, he refused to see me, and was quoted saying he "declined to accept it because...it would be unseemly in view of the tribunal." The petition was accepted by someone from the public affairs department of the force. Its existence was reported in the media; I don't know what the police department did with it.

I knew the petition itself would most probably do little to sway a decision in David's favor. But even if the police department had completely ignored it — which they may well have done — any project that encourages 57,000 people to get involved, even slightly, in the anti-abortion cause must be a good thing.

I hope that those 57,000 take their involvement much further. That many people, actively working against the ongoing slaughter of unborn babies, could make a very great difference.

There were other people who became even more personally involved. Some attended meetings such as the Choose Life Canada rally that honored David as Hero of the Year in Toronto.

Others turned out at demonstrations organized to protest the charges against David.

Right to Life and Campaign Life volunteers picketed 14 Division, demanding justice for David and, more importantly, for the unborn. There was consistent support by pro-life people outside the Bloor Street East tribunal offices as the tribunal was being held.

Within a day or two of David being charged, we received supportive and helpful phone calls from Jim Hughes of Campaign Life, and from Father Ted Colleton. We received flowers and phone calls from the Burnie sisters — Helen, Mary and Rita. Joe Borowski was soon in touch with us, offering support, as was Dan McCash.

During the final days of the trial period, as we awaited the verdict, Joe Scheidler, from Chicago, a well-known pro-life activist who works with the Pro-Life Action League, came to Toronto to give his personal support. David received a letter from Tom Buggeln, of the Maricopa County Deputies' Association in Arizona, offering him a job. We thought long and hard before deciding that God had another job for us, here in Toronto.

As well, David and I received many letters of support from all over the world. We genuinely appreciated them; they lifted us up, encouraged us, and gave us strength in days when strength was hard to find.

I have included a selection of those letters in the appendix at the back of this book.

Chapter Nine

On the stand

While our pro-life friends and supporters were demonstrating, picketing, attending rallies and signing petitions, the person who was facing the toughest challenge was seated in a fairly comfortable room, keeping warm and dry.

But if David had had his choice, he would much rather have been out on the street with a sign in his hand. My husband had far and way the most difficult job of all — defending his decision to refuse an order in a tribunal run entirely by police officers from the police department that had laid the charge of insubordination against him.

The charge was laid against David on April 8, 1987. He was put on restricted duty — the kind of desk job he still has (and still detests) as I write this — and he appeared before the first preliminary hearing on May 14, 1987.

The tribunal stretched on, with a number of breaks, for months, and the final decision by Superintendent Bernard E. Nadeau was not handed down until the end of January 1988.

The verdict was the worst possible decision, from our point of view. Despite an unofficial agreement reached between Police Force Prosecutor, Staff Inspector John Addison, and David's lawyer, Harry Black, that would have allowed David to remain on the force, but face some disciplinary action, Superintendent Nadeau decided that David must resign from the force within seven days, or be immediately dismissed.

All of that is now on hold, as David follows through the appeal procedure. His initial appeal is expected to be heard December 9, 1988.

There are some important, continuing concerns about the appeal process. The December appeal will be headed by June Rowlands, chairperson of the Metro Police Commission.

Last February, the **Toronto Star** reported: "An influential women's activist group has made a proposal to Health Minister Elinor Caplan to set up a women's health centre, including a full range of services from abortion to birthing, and possibly incorporating Dr. Henry Morgentaler's Harbord Street clinic."

According to the **Star,** one of the people backing this committee is June Rowlands. This does nothing to boost our faith that the next hearing will be more impartial than the first tribunal.

*****

My husband loved the work of a cop on the beat. I've already written about his now-lost dream of serving in Toronto's Vietnamese community. He earned his commendations through his work as a beat cop, and that kind of work was his reason for being a police officer, but now, for a year and a half, he's been assigned to a desk.

Incidentally, his current position includes a severely reduced salary, about $10,000 less than he was making before all of the changes came. We're still able to live, but his lower salary has made it much tougher to get by.

We have often been sent money to help us in our defence. We have kept none of it. Coincidentally, David discovered at one point that his mail was being examined at the police department (he often got letters of support mailed to the department), and they were watching carefully to see if he had ever kept any of the money. That would probably have led to additional charges.

We have either returned the money, or given it to Campaign Life. We're getting by on David's salary, and have used none of the gifts for our own purposes.

David now lives in a kind of police limbo. The department wants him gone, but the official procedure allows the appeals that he has launched. It seems as though the department has simply found boring jobs, well out of sight, for David to do. Maybe they're hoping he'll just go away.

I know my husband well enough to be certain that isn't how it is likely to happen.

******

The official transcript of the tribunal proceedings runs about 300 pages. The tribunal called twelve witnesses, as well as David himself. All of those witnesses were questioned by Mr. Black, Staff Inspector Addison and, often, Superintendent Nadeau.

It was clear all through the proceedings that the police department had a very different view from David about what had really taken place, and what the implications of David's action were.

There was, of course, a basic agreement. Everyone involved agreed concerning the essential fact that, on April 8, 1987, Police Constable David Packer had refused an order to take duty at the Morgentaler "clinic," on Harbord Street. They agreed that David had made that statement before three superior officers, one after the other. They agreed that his action had resulted in the charge of insubordination.

But that was just about where agreement ended.

****

Perhaps the most controversial disagreement that came out at the tribunal concerned a meeting held at 14 Division on January 3, 1986, more than a year before the incident that led to charges being laid against my husband.

On that occasion, the police officers at the Division were invited to meet with some of the high-ranking officers of the Department, including Deputy Chief William McCormack, who is responsible for field operations for the department.

That meeting had been called because the complexities of doing police work near the Morgentaler "clinic" were creating a lot of headaches and confusion for several of the officers involved. It was common knowledge that what was happening inside the "clinic" was illegal — freestanding abortuaries were definitely against the law — and yet, at the instruction of Ontario's Attorney General, no charges were being laid against Morgentaler and his colleagues.

The provincial government explained that this decision had been reached because Morgentaler had already been acquitted in trials by jury, which, in my opinion, indicates that a carefully-selected jury will, on occasion, be willing to completely overlook a really obvious example of the law being broken.

The entire issue had been sent to the Supreme Court of Canada, and the Attorney General had ordered the Metro police force to lay no more charges.

This had put a number of police officers in a very difficult situation. From time to time, officers had to appear in court to testify in cases where demonstrators had been arrested in front of the "clinic." The lawyers defending the protesters would, quite rightly, raise the issue that criminal activities were also taking place inside, but that this was being ignored by the police.

It actually wasn't the fault of the department — they were handcuffed by the Attorney General Ian Scott, who has the ultimate responsibility for police activities in the province of Ontario.

The officers involved were understandably confused. Deputy Chief McCormack came to meet with the officers of 14 Division to give some direction, and to answer their questions in a fairly informal setting.

This is where one of the basic disagreements of the tribunal comes in. David has a clear memory that, at that meeting, another officer raised a question about what police officers who were working the Morgentaler detail should do if they had genuine questions of conscience about it.

David remembers Deputy Chief McCormack saying that, if such questions of conscience came up, an accommodation would be made for those officers. David admitted at the tribunal that he could not quote everything the Deputy Chief said, exactly, but that "accommodation" was certainly part of the answer to the officers.

The Deputy Chief initially told the tribunal that he has no recollection of such a question and, therefore, denies that he gave such an answer; he did not remember any officer asking him a question regarding religious problems related to doing duty outside the Morgentaler "clinic."

However, at that point, David's lawyer, Mr. Black, told Deputy Chief McCormack that he intended to call evidence from four officers who were at that meeting, and who recalled the question being asked. Those officers — Staff Sergeant Grenville Dawkins, and Police Constables Michael Comars, Gino Pulla and Mario Di-Tomasso, took a huge risk, standing up for David by telling the truth, and we really appreciate their actions. The Deputy Chief subsequently recalled the question, although he insisted no indication was given that officers would be relieved of duty at the "clinic" on the grounds of conscience.

P.C. Pulla, in testimony to the tribunal, opened a window on what a police tribunal really is when he said that, before deciding to testify, he talked it over with his wife and a superior officer, wondering what the repercussions of his honest testimony might be concerning his career.

None of the three constables specifically remembered Deputy Chief McCormack using the term "accommodation" — something David remembers specifically — but all three told the tribunal that they were left with the impression that if officers had problems of conscience or religious conviction, concerning guarding the abortuary, that alternate arrangements could be made.

You can understand how important this particular issue is. If the Deputy Chief had said or implied that officers who could not, in good conscience, take duty at the "clinic" would receive an alternate assignment, nothing that David did was close to insubordination. If such was the case, he was, in fact, acting completely in accord with the instructions of his superior officers, and he had done nothing that was even subject to question.

David's lawyer was unable to convince the tribunal that the question and answer between Deputy Chief McCormack and an officer actually took place. I think that the decision of the tribunal rested largely on that disagreement.

I want to quote from David's evidence concerning this issue. He told the tribunal that he was present at the January 3, 1986 meeting. And he was asked if he remembers any of the particulars of the the questions raised in the question-and-answer part of the meeting.

His answer was:

"Yes, I do, of two. The first one asked that I remember was from a Police Constable who wanted to know what he should say under oath in court if he were asked whether he knew that abortions were taking place inside 85 Harbord Street and Deputy McCormack told him that of course he should tell the truth, that he does know it because it's a matter of public record, like it appeared it had come out of the mouths of the doctors in there themselves so, yes, of course he should say he knows."

David was asked about the second question he remembered. As he gave this answer, he admitted that he didn't remember the question or the answer, word for word, but he had a very clear memory of the circumstances, and of the nature of the question, and of the Deputy Chief's response to the question.

He told the tribunal:

"Police Constable Di Tommaso stood up and said he was a Catholic. He said he was having problems squaring guarding 85 Harbord Street with his religious beliefs and he wondered what could be done there to help him out, basically, and Deputy McCormack replied, and again, I can't remember it word for word, but to the effect that any officer having serious problems with guarding Morgentaler's abortuary would be accommodated.

"Now, the only word that I distinctly recall is the word "accommodated." He said it, there's no mistake in my mind, and it's stayed with me from that day to this day."

David was asked if he had considered putting the same question to the meeting with the deputy chief. He said that he had, and then was asked why he had not done so.

I'm very proud of my husband for his answer to that question. He didn't try to hedge, or explain that he was ready to ask it, but the other officer beat him to it. David is an honest man. There may be some in the department who doubt that, but they're wrong. There is no better evidence of his honesty than his answer to the question, "Why didn't you ask?"

David admitted:

"Because I didn't have the courage of P.C. Di Tomasso to ask that question, because there was a room full of guys that I worked with day in, day out, there was a Deputy Chief of Police, and apart from being handed my Police Graduation Certificate, I've never even met a Deputy Chief of Police.

"I was — to be kind to myself, I'd like to say that I was overawed by the Deputy and leave it at that, but I think a more honest picture is of someone talking to himself sitting there, sitting there, minute after minute, saying to himself 'ask the question — go ahead, ask the question now before it's too late,' and just not having the parts to stand up and ask him. I was sitting there. I was sweating so much trying to resolve this, trying to get the gumption to stand up and ask this question that I distinctly recall an enormous bead of sweat running all the way down my backbone, and being extremely uncomfortable as it made its way down there."

I know that same kind of sweat was running down his back as David spent his time on the witness stand. His appearances before the tribunal were the first time since the night before April 8 that he had trouble sleeping at night. As I've said, he does not like public gatherings of that kind, not at all, and he would have given anything to be anywhere else, just as long as it was not in that tribunal hearing room.

But his act of conscience had put him on that stand, with his actions and beliefs on the line, and he did not back down. I know that he told the truth, every minute on the stand. I know he remembers that meeting in January, 1986, and that David's recollection is accurate.

If the tribunal had believed him, there would be little question about the charges. David could not be accused of insubordination if a senior officer in the department had previously said that officers with problems of conscience concerning guarding the abortuary would be "accommodated."

******

During his long hours on the witness stand, David was questioned about every detail concerning the incident that led to his being charged. He was examined first of all by his own lawyer, Harry Black, and then by the prosecutor, Staff Inspector John Addison.

Of course, the approach of these two men was completely different — that's how the system works. For example, Inspector Addison challenged David's claim of a problem with conscience, since at the time David had not been a communicant member of the Roman Catholic Church.

It also became obvious that the issues concerning the meeting with Deputy Chief McCormack were not the only areas where memories of events or conversations were different.

A number of items of disagreement came up, and several more times, it was clear that if David's recollections could have been substantiated, he either would have been cleared, or his penalty would have been considerably less life-changing.

All I can say is, I believe David on every point. I don't know why other participants in the events have somewhat different stories.

I have to admit that David and I have differing views about the approaches taken by the prosecutor. David actually has nothing bad to say about him at all — he says Staff Inspector Addison was just doing his job, while I can't help feeling that the prosecutor was unfairly negative and almost brutal in his examination of my husband.

Be that as it may, as the tribunal neared an end, the Staff Inspector reached an agreement with David's lawyer, Mr. Black, that would have seen David found guilty and have initiated some disciplinary action. However, the agreement also stated that David would continue to be a constable with the Metro Toronto Police Department.

It was the tribunal officer, Superintendent Nadeau, who rejected that compromise agreement, and decided that David would have to leave the force within seven days. I'll talk more about those conclusions a couple of chapters from now.

******

One of the important issues raised earlier in David's testimony was the fact that he had, in reality, accepted duty at the Harbord Street abortuary on several previous occasions. David explained his decisions on those occasions, talking specifically about his night shift assignments to guard the "clinic":

"At the time I did them, I didn't see too much wrong with them, to be frank with you, and the reason is this. No abortions are happening at 85 Harbord Street during those times. It's just bricks and mortar and to my thinking when I did it, bricks and mortar can't be evil, they can't be good; they just are. So I was not taking part in any way in abortion.

"However, I'd like to point out right now that I think what I did on those occasions was to legitimize that building, that institution, in the eyes of anyone passing by on those occasions and I did it because I was in uniform, I was obviously a police officer, I was obviously there to guard the place and to any Tom, Dick or Harry just passing by, he would assume that no police officer in Metropolitan Toronto would be asked to go along with an evil person. He would assume by my being there that everything was okay and dandy at 85 Harbord Street because it's well known that the police don't protect murderers."

David was admitting that guarding the "clinic" building, even at night, was the wrong thing for him to have done. But he told the tribunal that the key moment when the evil of his involvement was forced upon him came during the one day shift he had done at the abortuary.

He testified:

"I believe I was there for at least four hours and I could have been there for more. I was there during the day, I was outside the front of the abortion facility and I was guarding the place just the way everyone else does when they go there. I was in a police car, I was facing west, I was watching the picketers walk up and down.

"If my memory serves me correctly, it was not a very nice day, and I thought they had a lot of conviction to be walking up and down there, for hours. I sat there just watching them walk up and down.

"A lady and a young girl about fifteen years old, I don't know but I believe from their age difference it could have been her daughter or her niece, I don't know the relationship, walked by my car and I paid no attention to them because they simply glanced across the road. I was on the other side of the road from the abortuary, and they looked across at the picketers at 85 Harbord as they went by, but they didn't seem to have too much keen interest.

"But about two, three minutes later they were back.

David at four

*With David at
Blenheim Palace,
Sir Winston Churchill's family home in England*

*With our
first baby,
Elizabeth
at Maternity Home in Reading, Berks, England*

*Happy
father,
David at
Niagara
Falls,
1978*

From left to right: Andrew, Mary, David, Elizabeth, Anne, Matthew, Julia

In the middle of the fuss . . . a peaceful occasion: David is confirmed by Father Daniel Utrecht

David has help blowing out candles on confirmation cake

Some of the picketers and counsellors at 85 Harbord

Joanne Dieleman ▼

Tom and Barbara Brown

Mike Lynch

Robert Hinchey in action

Leo Beecher

▲ *Dan McCash (left), Helen Burnie, David McDonald and other heroic activists have helped to save a number of babies under the most difficult circumstances.*

*"Arresting" photos of
Father Ted Colleton
and escorts*

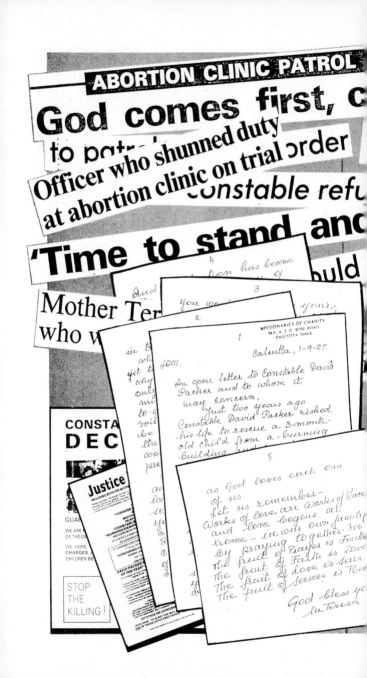

January 26, 1988. Superintendent Nadeau reading a "guilty" verdict to David.

Gerarda Savoie (centre) initiated petition signed by 57,000 people ◀

▲ *With Jim Hughes, President of Campaign Life Coalition.*

▲ *Inspector Neish receives petition for Police Chief Jack Marks.*

◀ *Meeting the press outside Police Headquarters.*

January 26, 1988 ▲
*Police Tribunal finds David
guilty of insubordination*

January 31, 1988 ▶
*At Queensway Cathedral,
David receiving "Hero of
the Year" Award from pro-
life Pastor Ken Campbell of
Choose Life Canada*

Joe Borowski and friends at 14 Division

▲ *With Joe Scheidler, President of Pro-Life Action League, Chicago and Jim Hughes*

Helen Burnie sums it up ▶

David picketing at MP's office in February 1988

Kurt Gayle and I co-ordinated the first Canadian Operation Rescue on October 29, 1988. Joan Andrews, American pro-life heroine and Joe Borowski were among participants

A Matter of Conscience

"They were walking back towards me and I began to think that here was a person being brought in for an abortion, and it clicked in me. I watched them. They crossed the road and they walked south through the laneway of the east side where the abortuary is and they disappeared from my view, and to this day I don't know if the girl went in for an abortion or not. I really don't know, but in my own mind I think she probably did and I had to think very hard of what was going on here.

"I had to think from my experiences at the Churchill Hospital, from intense reading I had done on the subject, brought on by something I had read in 1982, which told me unambiguously in very simple terms that there is no controversy among medical people, amongst the front line doctors, as to the fact that a child, person just like you and me is being killed at 85 Harbord Street at the rate of approximately fifteen every working day for money, by a doctor.

"It occurred to me that if this young lady were indeed in there having an abortion, at the moment I was thinking about it, a child, a person was being torn apart, and the only things separating me from this act of wilful murder were a couple of rows of bricks and an empty road.

"Without wanting to over-dramatize the situation, I felt myself honestly descending into hell, is the only way I can describe it as I sat there, because I was not an innocent party to this. That's all.

"I can't be a party to abortion. I can't collaborate in it being carried out."

David's testimony left no doubt as to his position on the subject. There was no room for "repentance" here — he hates abortion, he believes it is wrong, and he has come to see that guarding an abortuary is wrong. Giving credibility to that institution is, in David's view — and mine — collaboration with a deadly enemy.

After David had made his stand as clear as you have just read, I supposed there were only two choices: he could either be lauded as a man of conscience, or he could be rejected as an anti-abortion fanatic, or even as an opportunist who was grandstanding on an issue, either to gain public attention or, perhaps, simply to get out of a duty that no one in the entire Division ever claimed to be comfortable with.

David was closely examined on his religious beliefs, and on his views on abortion. It was clear that many of the police officials wanted to see him as a nut.

Chapter Ten

"In conscience, I couldn't do it"

The tribunal heard a lot about David's religious beliefs, and his views on abortion. He answered straightforwardly and honestly — there would have been no use in trying to downplay any of it, because we've found that people are either in agreement with our opposition to abortion, or they simply write us off as nuts.

I guess I understand that. If someone has been a supporter of abortion, or simply has remained silent about abortion, and then he or she actually confronts the reality of what is going on, that person is forced to go through a heart-rending change.

It can never be easy to admit that you have participated in, or closed a blind eye to, the wilful murder of human beings. But a lot of people are going to have to go through that process — which is terrible to begin, but very cleansing once you have truly turned around — if the destruction of tiny human lives is to stop.

David knew that he might be seen as a fanatic. But, on the stand, he simply told the truth about what he believes. I could not be more proud of my husband. He is a man of faith, of conscience, and of courage. The sort of man, I add editorially, who should make an absolutely ideal police officer.

It probably would have been much more convenient if David had been an ardent church-goer all his life. But that isn't the case.

I have always known that he had a basic, essential faith. As he told the tribunal:

"I don't know of a time in my life when I've not believed, firstly, that there is a God, that it is the God of the Christian Bible, that I was made by God and that, when I die, I'll be judged by that God on my life."

He also pointed out that our five children have all been raised as Catholics, and told the tribunal that, at the time he was on the stand, he was already taking religious instruction which has since brought him to his confirmation as a Roman Catholic.

I'm sure that some people must have concluded that David's involvement with the Roman Catholic Church was an opportunistic attempt to add credibility to his refusal to guard the "clinic." But I know that's not true; he had attended Mass with me for years, and his desire to be an involved part of the Church had been growing for a long time. His confirmation as a Catholic, on January 17, 1988, would have taken place whether or not he had been charged for refusing to guard the abortuary.

I also wonder why it's assumed that only a good Roman Catholic would have objections to abortion on the grounds of conscience. There are many, many people from various Christian churches, other faiths, and even people of no expressed religious faith at all who have joined hands to work against the evil of abortion.

Abortion is not wrong only if you're a Catholic. It seems clear to me that, when you know the facts, anyone has to conclude that abortion is a crime against humanity. All it takes to be opposed to abortion is to be a human being! There is a Christian argument against abortion, but there is also a compelling humanitarian argument.

David made that point clear in his testimony. He was asked about his views on abortion, and his involvement with the issue. Some of this story has been told earlier in the book, but here, you can read it in my husband's own words:

"Abortion is the murder of an innocent child, the gift of God.

"I can't imagine a time in my life when I would ever have been in agreement with abortion, but you have to understand that in my early years, abortion, like many of the weighty issues of this life, were not paramount in my thinking.

"My first direct involvement, for want of a better word, regarding abortion — the first time I had to consider the subject, was when I was working in the Churchill Hospital in Oxford, England, during summer vacation from Cambridge. I was working as a hospital orderly, as you call them over here, and my wife-to-be had become a Registered Nurse in the United States, at St. Vincent's Hospital in New York.

"She had gone to England, ostensibly to get a further nursing certificate, but I kind of suspect to see England, too, and she was also working at the Churchill Hospital as a registered nurse.

"Now, I came into contact (with abortion) while I was an orderly with the other orderlies, and one of them in particular, one day, had to take a garbage bag full of whatever detritus you get at hospitals, some of it human flesh, and his job was to take it from wherever he picked it up to the incinerator to be burned.

"Now, I wouldn't normally be interested too much in the garbage someone was throwing in an incinerator, but this chap mentioned that the bag had been moving as he was carrying it and he had taken it from the operating theatres, where I was aware abortions were carried out every day and routinely. Although he never opened the bag and he did throw it in the incinerator, he was extremely shocked.

"Also, my wife told me that she had seen aborted babies in a sluice room in the Churchill Hospital where they had been abandoned in — I don't remember if it was garbage receptacles or the sinks in the sluice room or whatever, but they'd just been — these dead babies were just tossed out and that had a very grave effect on me.

"From that time on, I was fully, intellectually, against abortion.

"However, you have to understand something here. I went back to university briefly, then I left, without a degree, to get married. I became a police officer concurrent with that and the abortion issue never impinged upon my life directly. I was never called upon to take any part at all in the whole process of abortion from beginning to end in any manner whatever.

"It was fully understood, it didn't even have to be articulated, that my wife would never countenance, herself, having an abortion, and until I came to Canada, more specifically until I came to 14 Division, it was something that, if you asked me at any time, 'What do you think about abortion,'" I'd have said, 'It's wrong.' I would have related my experiences and that would have been it.

"It still didn't impinge upon my life. My feelings had no practical application and they were in conflict with nothing."

But David found, like all of us who are involved in the struggle to end abortion, that being intellectually opposed was not enough. He became more and more involved. Together, we joined organizations opposed to abortion, began to take part in demonstrations, and gave as much money as we could to help to save the lives of unborn children.

As I have said, both of us read everything we could get our hands on, to educate ourselves. David told the hearing about the things he had learned from some of that material.

"I found out from (an) article that babies are being routinely starved to death in hospitals, and that the crime of infanticide is a pretty much an open secret amongst doctors. It took my mind to a very famous article called 'The Slippery Slope,' which a chap called Malcolm Muggeridge wrote in 1973. He predicted that as soon as human life lost its value, as soon as it could be taken arbitrarily through abortion, then what would follow from that would be euthanasia, that people, if they were considered worthless by a court, would be killed.

"When that article came out, it seemed incredible. It seemed incredible that the Slippery Slope could happen, and here it was nine years later that babies were dying now, born babies, and so it was going on.

"What this meant to me was that this enormous holocaust which was going on around me was the most frightening crime the world has ever known.

"Now, you say, how did I inform myself after that, what did that do to me? Well, I had to find out the medical facts. If you want to find out whether the earth is round, you read what the astronomers tell you. So I read what doctors say about abortion. I wanted to know if this was just a clump of cells that you scrape away, or whether it was a person; because, if it wasn't a person, if it wasn't a child being killed in abortion, then maybe there's some room for argument, and I expected some controversy amongst doctors.

"I expected five learned doctors to be saying, 'No, it's just cells,' and five learned doctors saying, 'This is a baby.'

"What I found was no medical controversy at all. Everyone, everyone agreed that this was an unborn baby. There was no argument. So, from that, I'd informed myself beyond, not just a reasonable doubt, but beyond any doubt, that a child is being killed in the womb during an abortion."

If I can leave David's testimony for a moment, I cannot write his observation without adding a comment of my own. It seems to me that this is the fundamental issue concerning abortion: is the fetus which is aborted a person, or is it a clump of cells?

Like my husband, when I first became involved in the issue, I expected that those who favor abortion would go to great lengths to prove that the fetus is not a human being. Instead, I found that no one offers any meaningful evidence at all that a fetus is anything except a small human being.

There is no evidence that anything except growth takes place from conception on. There is no magic moment when suddenly something is added to that being to make it a person. All that happens is growth. Everything that is present in an adult is present in some form in the tiniest unborn child.

This being the case, it is very confusing to me to encounter so many people who support the killing of these children. The facts are plain — we are killing human beings! Are we so callous in this society that we can eagerly, wilfully, take the lives of other people; innocent, helpless people at that? How can so many people ignore conclusive evidence that those beings that are being killed, every day, are human children?

I pray that people who are pro-abortion because of ignorance and lack of information will change their minds when they learn the truth. If not, we have slid further and faster down the Slippery Slope than I would ever want to imagine!

David explained to the tribunal that he was opposed to abortion long before he began to ally himself with the Roman Catholic Church. I think some of his critics have assumed that it went the other way, and that both his church affiliation and his stance against abortion are new elements in his life.

He made it clear that the Roman Catholic teaching against abortion was one of the things that attracted him to the faith that has been my spiritual home for my entire life. He told the hearing:

"I've known all along that the Roman Catholic Church is against abortion."

He said that once he had looked at the scientific evidence about abortion, he wanted to see what the church had contributed to the debate.

"I wanted to look at the religious side and see just what it was all about, what people were saying. I discovered that the Roman Catholic Church has said from its earliest times, unwaveringly, never changing, that abortion is the killing of a person that God has given into the womb."

****

A major part of David's time on the witness stand was taken up with a detail by detail account of the events of April 8, 1987. The information my husband supplied did not contradict the charge laid against him, but provided some details about the events of that day that seem to me to place his decision in a different light.

I think the facts, combined with the statement concerning "accommodation" that was attributed to Deputy Chief McCormack, indicate clearly that my husband did not commit an act of insubordination that day.

He was prepared to face the consequences if that interpretation was placed on his decision, because before God and his own conscience, he could no longer do duty at the Morgentaler "clinic," but I do not think his actions constituted insubordination toward his superior officers, or toward the Metro Toronto Police Department.

David told the tribunal that he first became aware that he might be assigned to guard the abortuary on March 16, 1987. That was the day he was told he was going on the Area Foot Patrol, the duty that included responsibility for foot patrol at the Morgentaler Clinic.

He testified that he did not immediately raise the question about duty there because he was privately hoping the problem might never come up. "I hoped I wouldn't have to do anything concerning the Morgentaler abortuary," he said.

It seems to me that, if nothing else, this proves that my husband had no intention of causing a controversy if one could possibly be avoided. If, by some unlikely chance, he had never been given another assignment to Harbord Street, none of this would have happened. David would have continued his efforts against abortion — as we always will — but it seems unlikely his conscience would have come into conflict with his duties as a Toronto police officer.

Somehow, though, I can't be sorry that this has all taken place. There are many things about this situation I do not enjoy, but I can see God's hand in this. At the most simple level, thousands, perhaps millions, of people have been exposed to the horror of abortion through David's situation.

I remember, at times in the past, realizing how much David enjoyed studying languages. I would occasionally feel guilty that he had left university to marry me, that he had cut short an academic career in an area of study that he loved.

But I no longer feel that way. If we had not married, if David had not left school and become a policeman, none of this would have happened. And despite the hassles and the minor hardships this has placed on us, I firmly believe that this is something that was meant to be.

And if we're doing God's will in this, it is exactly where David and I would want to be.

****

David's lawyer led him, point by point, through the moments of April 8. He reminded David that he had been assigned to the Morgentaler "clinic" during morning parade, at 7:30 a.m., but that David had not stated his unwillingness to go until five hours later.

David explained:

"Because the room was the Guardroom, the room we were paraded in. There were about thirty guys there, all getting their details, and if I had had the courage to say at that time, when he said what my detail was, 'Excuse me one second, I can't do that because my conscience won't let me do it,' two things would have happened.

"Firstly, I would have confronted the guy about as bluntly as walking over to him and hitting him with my night stick. I'd have put him on the spot right in front of all the other guys. Here's the Sergeant, there, rattling out details: you do this, you do that, you do the other, and suddenly when he gets to me, I put him on the spot, and he's the supervisor, and firstly, that's not the done thing.

"You don't confront a supervisor, as far as I'm concerned, in front of a group of police constables, and put him in a hard place.

"The second thing that would have happened would be that I would have used up all the courage because I'm a very quiet, shy person. I'd have used up all the courage that (I found) the night before, when it seemed very obvious to me that I might have to go to the "clinic."

"I'd been tossing and turning and charging myself up to have the courage to refuse to do it, because it is so utterly wrong. In the grey light of day, when a lot of that evaporated, for me to stand up suddenly with the courage, in front of all these guys I'd worked with, and say that, was something I didn't have.

"I didn't have the parts to do it."

You know, it almost hurts me to write these words. My husband did one of the bravest things I've ever heard of, yet throughout his testimony at the tribunal, he talks about his lack of courage. That says more to me about his basic humility, than it does about any absence of "parts." In my books, David is a brave, brave man. He's willing to face whatever comes, because of his act of conscience. There aren't many people out there with that much guts.

****

In his testimony, David had already disagreed with the Deputy Chief of Police concerning what happened at the January, 1986 meeting concerning the Morgentaler "clinic."

Now, he was asked about a conversation he had had with Staff Sergeant Alan Griffiths, of 14 Division. He had met with the staff sergeant when David was first assigned to the Area Foot Patrol — that was one of Staff Sergeant Griffiths' responsibilities.

The staff sergeant had already told the tribunal that his meeting with David had included discussion of patrol at the Morgentaler "clinic," a subject that was a normal part of the staff sergeant's introduction to anyone assigned to that particular patrol. When the subject of patrol at the "clinic" was raised, said Griffiths, David had offered no objection to that assignment.

If that were accurate, that would obviously have been an important strike against my husband. If, as testified, he had been given the chance to comment, in a discussion, one-on-one, with his superior officer, and had not done so, then his actions on April 8 could easily be seen as the product of a strange, spur-of-the-moment decision, or as the confrontational act of a trouble-maker.

But David, under oath, disagreed with the testimony of his superior officer.

Mr. Black asked him:

"You've heard from Staff Sergeant Griffiths yesterday that when you were first assigned to the Foot Patrol, he called you in as is his practice with all new members of the Force that are at 14 Division who are assigned to the Community Foot Patrol, and he had a discussion with you and he says that at that time he told you that part of your duties would be the detail at the Morgentaler Clinic, and that you said nothing. What do you say as to that evidence?"

David replied:

"That's incorrect. He didn't mention it.

"...Now, to be fair to him, before he spoke with me, I knew that part of the duties on the Area Foot Patrol during day shift was to guard that place, okay? I don't want to be unfair to the guy. He didn't tell me at that meeting, but I did already know. At that meeting, I'll tell you what was covered.

"I went into the C.I.B. Staff Sergeant's office and he said: 'Welcome to the Foot Patrol a bit belatedly. How are things, and what do you have to expect?' And to make a long story short, we spent the whole time talking about a certain oriental group of people that I was heavily involved in working on, and that was the extent of it.'

David says that his meeting with his superior on the Foot Patrol was entirely concerned with his work in the Vietnamese community. That seems very likely to me — I've already written about his passion for that particular area of police work. But it is certainly significant that the subject of the Morgentaler "clinic" did not come up.

In contrast to the earlier testimony by the staff sergeant, David had not ducked an opportunity to ask for relief from that duty. Mr. Black asked David why, if he knew that the abortuary was part of the Foot Patrol's area, David did not raise the issue himself in the meeting with the Staff Sergeant.

Again, he was honest:

"I don't know. I knew it was very likely, but I didn't know I was going to be (assigned there), and I hoped I wouldn't have to be. Why speak about it if possibly it will never happen?"

******

On the charge sheet against David, my husband is accused of refusing to take the assigned duty to the Morgentaler "clinic." His comments about his decision, as quoted in the charge sheet, are:

"You could not stand by a place that was killing babies; the detail was not a lawful order, and you would not do it."

The charge sheet says that when Staff Sergeant Alan Griffiths gave him a direct order to attend outside the "clinic," "you replied, 'I respectfully refuse. I don't think it's a lawful order.'"

Finally, the charge states that when Superintendent John Getty repeated the order, "you replied, 'I must respectfully decline.'"

David denies none of this. But in his testimony before the tribunal, he added many significant details that make it very clear he was not trying to create a controversy. He suggested alternatives, and he stated that this was a question of conscience — an issue that had been raised, according to my husband, at the meeting with Deputy Chief McCormack.

Like all police officers, David keeps a detailed notebook on the events in which he is involved. Those notes are always made as soon after any incident as possible, so testimony about whatever occurs during a police officer's duty can be as accurate as possible.

In giving his testimony, David was not working from memory of what happened months before. He consulted his notes frequently.

The following is taken from my husband's account of what really happened from 12:30 p.m. onward, on April 8, 1987:

"I told him (Sergeant Crawford, his duty sergeant) that I couldn't do the detail of guarding the clinic in the afternoon as I had been slated to.

"I told him that it was operating outside the law, and that babies are being killed inside. Then I asked him if I could work any other detail, whatever. I told him I thought it was a crummy detail. I understood that, that guys didn't like doing it, and I wanted to stress to him that I wasn't trying to slide out of a crummy detail, okay? I asked him to give me another order, any other crummy detail going. I said to him: 'Give me a crummy detail. Give it to me every day, you can do whatever you like. Just don't send me to this place because my conscience won't allow me to guard a place where they're killing babies.'"

According to David's testimony, Sergeant Crawford consulted with his superior officer,

Staff Sergeant Griffiths. David was called into meet with both of them.

Mr. Black asked David, "So he (Staff Sergeant Griffiths) ordered you to do the detail, and what did you say?"

David testified, "I told him I couldn't. I told him that in conscience I couldn't do it."

David's claim of conscience was not reported on the charge sheets, and some testimony at the tribunal from superior officers suggested that he had never mentioned his conscience.

I don't know if that detail made much difference to the verdict. But I do know that David was not just ducking a detail he didn't want to do, nor was he trying to create a hassle.

My husband simply could not, in good conscience, obey an order to guard an abortuary where blatantly illegal and deadly activities were going on.

Whatever the final outcome of this, I know he could have done nothing else. The testimony of Father James Wingle, outlined in the next chapter, makes it clear that, from the viewpoint of the Church and, more importantly, if David wanted to do the will of God, he had no choice.

Chapter Eleven

"Human life is sacred"

One of the most important witnesses for the defence at the tribunal was Father James Wingle, of St. Augustine's Seminary in Scarborough. Father Wingle was asked to give evidence about the position of the Roman Catholic Church, and thus what the position of a practising Roman Catholic should be, concerning the key issues facing the tribunal.

David was not, at the time he was charged, nor at the time of the tribunal, a member of the Roman Catholic Church. But he was a faithful adherent; he had been attending church with me for years, and at the time of the tribunal, was receiving instruction from a priest, leading to membership in the Church.

Last January, David was confirmed as a Roman Catholic (since he was baptized as an Anglican, he did not need to be baptized again). He is now a communicant member of the Church, something that delights me, because we can share our faith on yet another level. I have remained in the Roman Catholic Church since my personal return to faith.

Father Wingle was an excellent witness. Ironically, there is little to indicate that his testimony had much effect on the decision of the tribunal. However, he stated his case so well, that I want to quote his testimony from the tribunal at length. Father Wingle made it very clear what a good Catholic Christian should do, faced with the decisions that David had to make.

Father Wingle was asked, early in his testimony, to outline the Church's position on abortion. His answer was detailed but direct:

"The Catholic Church teaching from the Scriptures, from the Bible, teaches that God is the author of human life, that God created human life and creates human life, that because of that creation by God, human life is sacred.

"The first sin after the original disobedience was in fact, killing, or a sin against human life, the sin of Cain, as we know from the Scriptures. The Church teaches that human beings have an obligation to respect life, to reverence it and to safeguard it. This obligation, which individual persons have, falls in a special way on the State to protect particularly the innocent and helpless life. Of course, I think we can say in fact there is no more innocent and no more helpless form of life than the life of a child in its mother's womb.

"Consequently, there is an obligation to uphold the dignity of life and respect for it. The Church clearly holds that the direct intervention to take human life, to kill innocent life, is abominable and is utterly, morally wrong. The further teaching is that no person may in any way lend his or her consent to such activity, whether or not it's permitted or not permitted according to the laws of human society."

Father Wingle left absolutely no doubt as to where the Catholic Church stands on abortion. It is, in his terms, "an abomination." He also made it clear that the Church believes that responsibility concerning abortion goes far beyond those most directly involved — anyone who "consents" to abortion also bears responsibility for the evil that is committed by those involved in the act itself.

The priest also pointed out, very directly, that the moral wrongness of abortion does not change with the laws of the country. David's lawyer asked him to further detail Christian teaching on abortion. His answer was short and to the point:

"Abortion is offensive, profoundly offensive to God as the author of life, but it is also a violation of human reason in that it flies in the face of the human good of life and therefore is in violation both of God's law and of human reason."

In that statement, Father Wingle took opposition to abortion far beyond the boundaries of the Catholic Church. He presented an idea that David and I have held for a long time: abortion is the killing of defenceless human beings; religious faith aside, abortion is therefore a violation of basic human reason.

David had asked to be excused from duty guarding the Morgentaler "clinic" because his conscience would not allow him to guard a place that was killing babies. The lawyer asked Father Wingle about the teaching of the Catholic Church concerning human conscience.

"The teaching on conscience has developed over the centuries, developed very clearly. Conscience is, in a manner of speaking, the final court of appeal between the individual and God, and conscience, of course, has to be properly formed and informed, both according to the revealed truth of God, as we've received it in the Holy Scriptures and as the Church teaches it, and conscience must also take into account the operation of reason, of properly functioning human reason."

The witness agreed with a statement from the lawyer, that a Catholic must act in accordance with his conscience.

But he added to that. Father Wingle said:

"This binding nature of conscience pertains not only to members of the Roman Catholic Church, but to all men and women of reason and good faith. The Church's teaching on conscience is that, ultimately, the dignity of the human person rests on conscience, on a respect for conscience, that this freedom and intelligence with which human beings are gifted is a constitutive part of what contributes to human dignity."

Harry Black, David's attorney, pressed this point with Father Wingle. It was obviously very important to David's defence of his own decision to refuse the assignment at the Morgentaler "clinic."

Mr. Black asked:

"Is a person then, in his own conscience, able to come to an opinion as to whether or not a law or a legal state of affairs is moral or immoral?"

Father Wingle's answer is very interesting:

"That's precisely the kind of judgment that conscience renders. When conscience operates properly, it weighs all the factors of a situation. It weighs if there is any clear point of revelation, of something that we know from God, which we call theological revelation, and of the Church's teaching.

"Conscience takes that into account as its guiding norm. It takes into account the obligations of the situation, the obligations that may be there from a variety of sources and the particular factors of any given situation, and weighs all of those factors together such that the person reaching a judgment is then obliged, once that person has reached a judgment of certitude as to his or her obligation, the person must comply with that decision that he or she has reached, in fault of which he or she acts against himself."

The lawyer asked Father Wingle if a person need ever decide to follow his conscience in defiance of a law of the state. Father Wingle cited a basic principle as guidance in such a situation.

He said, "If there is no justice in the law, it loses, in the moral sense, its obligatory force."

He followed that with an example:

"Let us say for instance there's the obligation of a citizen to respect the law of the land with regard to property rights, trespass to property. If a further obligation is interposed there above that obligation, let us say the protection of or the enabling of the protection of human life, if a person is dying in a building, there would be a positive obligation to respect the higher order, the higher law there, that is, the regard for life itself above respect for property rights. In other words, a higher obligation could vitiate the prescription of a lower obligation."

Father Wingle then made an interesting point:

"In the democratic state," he said, "one hopes that the legislature creates as much space as is reasonably possible to respect the consciences of citizens."

Mr. Black then presented Father Wingle with a "hypothetical" situation that paralleled David's. Mr. Black put it this way:

He spoke of "a police officer whose order is to attend outside an abortuary and to keep the peace, and let's assume that that is, according to the civil law, a lawful order. Is it possible, according to the teachings of the Church, for that person to view even that limited role, of maintaining the peace and protecting incidents on the sidewalk, accidents on the roadway, damage to property — is it possible that a person, according to the true teachings of the Catholic Church, could view that as morally objectionable?"

Father Wingle agreed that the officer could be right in choosing not to follow that order. His lengthy explanation is as follows:

"I must say the complexity of that situation is obviously intense and I would and do have the greatest sympathy, empathy for a public official, police officer or whoever, to be put in that situation.

"In fact, if I may offer you the opinion, it seems to me there is a rather ironic, perhaps even schizophrenic situation presented there where the law of the land, which we know clearly does not permit free-standing abortion clinics. If such an operation is in progress, an officer of the law knows that the activity is occurring within that facility in contravention of the law, his sworn duty is to uphold the law. I don't think there's any question about that; that's not a question of moral teaching as such; that's, I think, a question of judgment, of sound reason."

(I want to step in, in the middle of Father Wingle's testimony, to underscore the point he has just made. He went much farther than suggesting that an officer should have to right to absent himself or herself from duty at the "clinic." He insists that the police officers assigned to the Morgentaler abortuary not only have the right of conscience to refuse, but that officers on duty there should have arrested those who are performing abortions, which was clearly a criminal act under the law as it then stood).

Father Wingle continued, "The second point is, you referred to a police officer receiving an order from his legitimate superior. Any police officer, any official is obliged to receive and adhere to the orders of his legitimate superiors, provided they do not put him in conflict with the moral order, with what is morally good.

"To go further in the scene that you paint for me, it is quite conceivable that if an individual in the circumstances you've described, receiving an order which at first glance is quite a legitimate order, that it's to keep the peace, which is a good thing, but in the totality of the circumstances of the case, if the individual officer in question sees that there are a variety of other factors, in this instance his clear knowledge or at least his assumed knowledge that the law is being broken, the law of man, and more significantly, the law of God is being violated in a fundamental way, he might well consider himself bound not to associate himself with that activity and his obligation and conscience then would be to distance himself as far as reasonably possible from that primary commission of evil and illegality.

"In concrete I would say he would be obliged to have recourse to his legitimate superiors to explain as far as he's capable his situation, and to ask for consideration. If he can't receive it, then he cannot violate, if his conscience is certain and clear, he cannot violate his conscience without committing a great evil."

In other words, David did the right thing. We had known that all along, but when Father Wingle made it very clear in the tribunal, it served to strengthen our conviction that David not only made the right choice — in fact, according to his conscience and his Christian faith, he had no choice at all!

Later in his testimony, Father Wingle again stressed the responsibility of a Christian to make decisions in good conscience.

He told the tribunal:

"Every human person who is rational and capable has to arrive at his or her own judgment of all of those facts. I'm not saying that he or she can ignore the teaching of the Church, but he or she must listen to the dictates of right reason, listen to the dictates of the Scriptures, the Bible, as the Church teaches from the Bible, and must do what he or she holds there in good conscience to be what is good and true."

During Father Wingle's testimony, Mr. Black introduced as evidence a statement on abortion issued by Gerald Emmett Cardinal Carter, the Archbishop of Toronto. The statement left no doubt as to the position of the Catholic Church concerning abortion.

It says:

"It must in any case be clearly understood that a Christian can never conform to a law which is in itself immoral and such is the case of a law which would admit in principle the licitness of abortion, nor can a Christian take part in a propaganda campaign in favor of such a law or vote for it. Moreover, he may not collaborate in its application."

That statement leaves little room for a Christian of good conscience to tolerate abortion in any way! If every Catholic, and every Christian who agrees with that statement, worked actively in the spirit expressed in it, we would have an enormous army fighting the presence of abortion in our land!

After Mr. Black had concluded his examination of Father Wingle, the witness was cross-examined by Staff Inspector Addison, the Police Force Prosecutor. One of his questions raised the issue of "sin."

Staff Inspector Addison asked:

"Relative to the hypothetical question my friend gave you, if a Roman Catholic of such strong beliefs as my friend described did duty at an abortuary as my friend described, would this be considered a sin by the Catholic Church?"

Father Wingle replied:

"When you raise the question 'sin', you've ceased to talk any longer at the level of, shall we say, public morality. You're talking about a personal judgment about this or that individual, whether he or she has sinned. Ultimately, God alone knows what freedom exists in a man's or woman's heart, and therefore God alone can adjudicate whether or not...our situation before God is sinful.

"To make that specific judgment that a person has sinned would mean that I would know that the person knew that what he or she was doing was greatly wrong, or at least substantially wrong, that he or she willed to do it, and that he or she fully proceeded without any force or any secondary compelling factors towards that action. If those conditions were all met then we would say that a sin was present, yes. Someone who knowingly, willingly engaged in something that he or she knew to be evil and did it as evil."

There has been a lot of debate, throughout this whole issue, about the question of conscience. Opinions seem to vary from those expressed by some newspaper columnists — that a conscience is a definite handicap to a police officer, who should just get on with his job, no questions asked, please — to those who believe a good cop must be a person of conscience, and must follow his or her conscience.

That, of course, is what got David into trouble.

Staff Inspector Addison raised this issue with Father Wingle. The prosecutor asked,

"We've discussed this hypothetical police officer of very strong religious beliefs; we've also discussed duties he may be called upon to do, has been ordered to do....Do you think the police profession is a good place for that type of person?"

Father Wingle left no doubt as to his view.

"I would hope ardently that every police officer would have recourse to a fully formed conscience, and would be very sensitive and responsive to his or her conscience," he said.

The prosecutor asked if, in such an officer, his conscience may overrule his duties.

Father Wingle agreed that such might be the case. "It is conceivable that the truth, as it impinges on an individual police officer's conscience, would put him or her in conflict with his duties....

"A case, a famous case comes to mind as a bit of leisure reading I've been doing. The case of a man during the Second World War, Franz Jegerstatter, he's an Austrian peasant, who found himself in conflict with the law of his country, of Austria after the Nazi takeover of his government. He was summoned to do duty in the Nazi army and he resisted.

"The officials I think could be described as having been otherwise inexplicably kind to him; they took him to Berlin, pleaded with him to take secondary duty as a stretcher-bearer or something to that effect, and he reasoned, no, he couldn't do that either, that even bearing a stretcher in that instance would be freeing up another German citizen to participate in something he held to be profoundly immoral.

"The man was executed in Berlin in 1943. I think the man is a hero, frankly."

By the time Father Wingle had finished his time on the stand, I was so glad he had been called as a witness. Even if his testimony had no impact on the tribunal, everything he said gave further strength to David's conviction, and to mine, that David had done the right thing.

Just as Father Wingle had described, David had been a faithful Christian in rejecting abortion, in following in conscience, in putting his belief in God's law above his loyalty to the laws of the state.

Whether or not the police department agreed, by Father Wingle's definition, my husband was a loyal, faithful, good cop.

Chapter Twelve

Quit or be fired!

At the end of January, 1988, the decison of the tribunal was announced: Police Constable David Packer was to resign from the Metropolitan Toronto Police Force within seven days, or he would be dismissed.

The reaction was immediate, on several fronts. David and his lawyer, Mr. Black, decided to appeal the decision. That appeal procedure would leave David on limited duty for months — perhaps years — longer than he had already been, but my husband felt he had no choice. He knew he had done what was right, and saw no justice in being punished for following the dictates of his conscience.

In addition to launching an appeal according to the official structure of the police department, David and Mr. Black also decided to appeal through the Ontario Human Rights Commission, with their case there resting on the issue of wrongful dismissal.

As I write this, we are still waiting for the various appeal procedures to get underway. We have sometimes wondered if the entire thing is being ignored for some reason! David is working at a desk job with the Toronto police department.

There were many expressions of support after the tribunal's verdict was announced. Most, of course, came from supporters of the pro-life movement, but even within the police community, many seemed shocked at the severity of the penalty.

Paul Walter, president of the Metro Toronto Police Association, told the newspapers that "I think the penalty imposed is one that's beyond comprehension. I think the penalty that he received is one that is far in excess of the normal disciplinary rules."

Walter, who has actually been publicly critical of David's action, said that a five-day suspension would have been more appropriate, followed by David's re-assignment to a division that does not cover the Morgentaler "clinic."

The police association also pledged to give David whatever financial support he needs to appeal the verdict. His legal costs for the original tribunal were also paid by the association, as is customary for an officer in such a situation.

******

The verdict came from Superintendent Bernard Nadeau, who had conducted the tribunal. As I have mentioned before, the decision ignored a proposed agreement worked out between the police prosecutor and David's attorney, Mr. Black.

Superintendent Nadeau was extremely outspoken in bringing down his ruling. He said, "I was not impressed by Constable Packer on the witness stand. I found him arrogant, insolent and argumentative when he was unable to control the questions. "

He charged that there was no possibility of rehabilitation, in David's case. He said, "I cannot, in view of your lack of remorse, see how you can continue as a police officer in this force."

The superintendent was quoted as asking, "How can the chief of police run a force when officers choose their own details?"

He said that David is "among a group of police officers who insist on making their own rules and telling the force what to do." He insisted that chaos and anarchy would prevail if other officers acted as David had done.

Superintendent Nadeau stated that there was no evidence that David's religious beliefs conflicted with the assignment he had refused.

****

It seems clear, from the Superintendent's comments, that there was little chance that David would have been able to convince the tribunal that his decision was the right one, that a police officer had the right to obey his own conscience.

The comments following the announcement of the verdict indicate that David's only hope would have been to say, "I was wrong. I admit it. I'll never do something like that again."

That, he cannot say.

What has been seen as arrogance in my husband is, in reality, conviction. David is not an arrogant man, but he is a man of principle, a man who will not compromise on an issue as important as this one. According to Father Wingle, a witness before the tribunal, David would have been imperilling his soul had he ignored the teaching of the scriptures, the Church, and the dictates of his conscience. David has frequently made that very statement in speaking engagements in the last year, and in saying so, he is standing on firm doctrinal ground, according to the teaching of the Catholic Church.

Immediately after the verdict was announced, David explained why he would not quit the department: "A person resigns if he has done something wrong," he said. "I will not resign."

Instead, he launched his appeal. The appeal process goes first to the Metro Police Commission, then, if that is unsuccessful, to the Ontario Police Commission and the Divisional Court.

It's going to be difficult. David continues to work in the Metro Toronto Police Department, the same department that employs the superior officers with whom he disagreed under oath. An appeal will mean going over all the same ground, again.

But he had to appeal. First, it is necessary because a principle is at stake: that a police officer must be able to follow his or her conscience. If there is no room for personal conviction, what kind of officers will the department be putting on the streets?

In fact, we are delighted to discover that the Pro-Life Nonviolent Action Project, based in New York City, has developed a set of proposed guidelines for police departments which acknowledge the right of police officers to follow the guidance of their consciences.

The report from the project includes a "Conscience clause for police and law enforcement officials." It reads:

"No police officer or other law enforcement official shall be ordered to obey or to enforce any order which that officer believes, in conscience, contrary to his own religious and moral principles.

"In furtherance of that official rule of conduct, that officer may request and be granted relief of such an order without prejudice of any kind or any adverse change of assignment or duties, or adverse performance merit review or rating, or adverse action on his merits in pay or assignment.

"In the event of any alleged adverse recommendation or discrimination against such officer, that action will be subject to immediate review and held in abeyance until resolved under proper police department internal regulations and under guidelines established with the Fraternal Order of Police in such matters."

I have to admit that I think it is unlikely that the Metro Toronto Police Department will adopt such a regulation in the near future. But it rests on plain common sense, and would make a wonderful contribution to internal police morale. It would also allow prospective officers to join the force who might be having second thoughts after what David has gone through.

Of course, in some cases, the Metro department has used that kind of reasoning. I'm referring to the decision that Sikh officers, who must wear a turban as part of their religious observance, may be excused from motorcycle duty because they cannot wear the turban and a motorcycle helmet at the same time.

From the time that decision was made, both David and I have applauded the common sense of the exemption. It's important, in our multi-cultural city, to have officers representing all of the groups who make up the community of Toronto. If no exemptions had been made, there might have been no Sikh police officers.

But we feel that the same provisions should be made for officers who have genuine questions of conscience about duty at an abortuary. So far, the powers that be in the department have not understood the similarity in the two situations. Sadly, a significant number of Roman Catholic officers are accepting that duty. I cannot believe that none of them find this weighing on consciences.

******

As I reflect on the outcome of the tribunal, I have to confess that it makes me sad at times. It is clear to me that David was not believed, on many points. Yet I know my husband was telling the truth — it's not in his nature to lie.

It also seems to me that Father Wingle's testimony had little or no impact. I'm not sure why that is, unless the police department somehow sees itself as above or beyond religious considerations. If that's true, they have only just begun to encounter the kind of problems that will come up, because I have to believe that David Packer is not the only cop with a conscience in the city of Toronto.

Of course, we also wonder why superior officers gave testimony that, according to David's careful notes, did not accurately represent the facts.

I suppose all these questions may resurface during the appeal procedure. It's the only way to go, but it's hard to be thrilled about many more months of controversy. But we will do it, simply because it's something that has to be done.

The one issue that was apparently ignored in the findings of the tribunal, is the issue of abortion. I know that the tribunal was not called to make the definitive decision about abortion in Canada, but to suggest that David's religious faith and his views on abortion are not important to his decision to refuse duty at the illegal abortuary seems to me to miss a crucial point.

The fact is, police officers in Toronto were called on to enforce the law selectively. While they were ordered to guard the "clinic," and to "keep the peace" there, which included, on occasion, the arrest of pro-life demonstrators, they were told to turn a blind eye to blatantly criminal activities going on inside the "clinic," where children were being killed.

As Father Wingle suggested, a police officer acting in good conscience would have felt compelled in his or her heart, to enter the abortuary and make arrests.

Toronto's cops could not do that, because of the decision of the province's Attorney General. That kind of decision-making contributed much to the situation my husband found himself in.

The tribunal is over. The appeals go on.

And we are going on with life, a life that has been changed drastically since those charges were laid against David. My husband has been called a "hero", honored my many groups and, to his continuing horror, invited to be a guest speaker to large groups of people.

And I lost a baby.

Chapter Thirteen

The epidemic of blindness

As you have gathered, much that is both good and bad has come out of this situation we've been living in for the past year and a half. We've been given a public forum and important opportunities to talk about the plight of the unborn children in our land. Perhaps, already, some lives have been saved, because people have been forced to think about the horror of abortion after reading of David's situation.

And it may be that, as he's taken all the courage he could find, and forced himself to stand before crowds of listeners, some people have been encouraged to become involved, or to get more involved, in this absolutely important issue.

We hope and pray that this is true.

David and I were both very humbled — as well as surprised — when, on June 24 of 1988, he was presented with a very high honour, the William Kurelek Pro-Life Award. (I later discovered that most of our friends knew about the award in advance. We heard absolutely nothing until the evening of the presentation).

The award states that it is given "in recognition of an outstanding contribution to the development of respect and appreciation for the dignity and worth of human life."

David continues to insist he is not a hero. But he is certainly honoured to be a part of the most important fight in the world, the fight for the lives of the children.

We believe that much that is good is coming, and will continue to come, out of the struggle that David and our family have gone through over the past months.

But it hasn't all been wonderful.

David and I have five children, whom we love very much: Elizabeth, Matthew, Andrew, Mary and Julia. They range in age, as I write, from 11 down to two.

I love children. I'm also a practising Catholic, and that precludes the use of birth control. Those two facts are a fortunate combination in my life.

Early in 1988, I became pregnant again. I had previously suffered two miscarriages, and those experiences had been among the hardest times I have ever had to face. This third miscarriage may have been especially hard because, although our faith remains strong — in fact, it seems to grow stronger, every day — this has been a period of intense stress, in many ways.

I believe that the pressure of David's status and appeal, and of all the public attention, was one of the factors contributing to the miscarriage of my baby.

Initially, I went through a time of intense grief. It was just about that time that the idea of this book was presented to me by our friends at Campaign Life, and I didn't even want to think about it. My first reaction was, "No way."

But Jim Hughes, president of Campaign Life, has a unique knack of being very compassionate and very insistent at the same time. He quickly convinced me of the potential value and usefulness of this book, and I agreed to proceed with the project.

I've realized, since coming through the most

intense stages of the grief that losing our baby caused, that there is much I can learn from the three miscarriages.

Perhaps, most importantly, it helps me in some ways to feel deep sympathy for women who have undergone an abortion.

It will not surprise you when I tell you how utterly, completely I am in opposition to abortion. I believe that the killing of our children is the most heinous crime in society today, one of the most criminal acts in the history of civilization.

But I also feel very deep compassion for women who have co-operated in the killing of their babies.

I believe that many women who have abortions do so as though through a fog. They are often terribly weighted down by what they perceive to be a horrible situation. Having a baby is never a horror, but our society has done so much to convince people that what should be a miracle is, instead, a tragedy.

And many women who choose to have abortions are in genuinely unfortunate situations.

There is also the fog of pro-abortion propaganda, lies and half-truths that completely confuses many people about this issue. Those whom David calls "the lunatics" have done so much to obscure the truth, to hide the reality that the being that is to be killed is a living human baby. They have presented abortion as a legitimate option, as a way to solve an inconvenient situation.

So many women who walk into the Harbord Street abortuary, or who have an abortion in a Canadian hospital where doctors are committing acts as evil as any done on Harbord Street, seem really to be unaware of the enormity of what they are about to do. Our society has developed a willing case of total blindness, and it seems to be contagious. It's one of the most serious epidemics we face.

But I know, from talking to many women who have gone through the experience, that the horror, the guilt and the shame set in later. Eventually, almost any woman will realize what has happened. All of the propaganda terms about "fetuses", "terminated pregnancies" and "procedures" disappear. The truth comes, always in these terms: "I've killed my baby!"

And, although I can never fully comprehend what it is like to bear responsibility for that deliberate act, I can deeply sympathize with any woman over the loss of her child.

Because three times, I have experienced the grief of the death of my own babies. I did not see them, or hold them in my arms, but I carried them within me and, like every mother, I knew them. I loved them. And they died.

I even know the guilt of feeling responsible for the death, in some way. After a miscarriage, you always wonder if, somehow, it was your fault: "Did I do something wrong? Was it something I did that precipitated this? If I had done things differently, would my baby be all right?"

I think about that, and then I think about the enormous load of guilt that must be carried by women who have actually paid for the death of their child, and then, only after the terrible fact, they have come to realize what they have done.

That's why abortion is so cruel to the women involved. They are at a very vulnerable point in their lives. They may have been sick, and they are very emotionally distraught. And a mother, in panic and in haste, goes to a doctor who kills the child.

She then has an entire life to repent of her action. It's a terrible price, for everyone involved.

The pro-life movement has often been accused of focusing on preventing abortion, without ever presenting alternatives. I don't think that's true — the organization called Birthright has been around for a long time, doing an important and compassionate job — helping pregnant women who are in difficult circumstances. They provide an important service, an alternative for women who might be considering aborting their babies. Birthright presents a perfect alternative.

It's important to remember that there are always alternatives. Aborting a baby is never a real answer to a difficult situation. It only involves trading one short-term trauma for a life of misery, and that at the cost of the life of a child.

Perhaps one thing we need to focus on more, in pro-life, is helping women who have had abortions. If you think about it, you may realize that we are better placed to help than almost anyone else.

If a woman has had an abortion, and then is burdened down with guilt, where can she go to get help and receive forgiveness? To the doctor that did the abortion? Hardly.

That doctor has a vested interest in maintaining the deadly fantasy, that abortion is a legitimate act. Therefore, he or she will only tell the woman who has had the abortion that she has nothing whatsoever to feel guilty about.

Does that help the woman who is genuinely burdened down with guilt? Not at all.

Can she go to her friends, those who have encouraged her to have her abortion? Can she go to her family, if they are the ones who supported her terrible decision? Of course not — again, all of these people will either have to convince her she has nothing to be guilty about, or they will have to face their own personal guilt in the matter.

And people in our society have become masters at avoiding guilt — at least, on the surface. Underneath, I believe, many people in our day are being torn to emotional shreds.

We in the pro-life movement best understand the woman's guilt. We agree with her that she has done a terrible thing. But many of us in the movement also understand the forgiveness of God, that there is no sin too great for Him to forgive. All of us have done some terrible things in our lives, and have survived only through the mercy of God.

We can stand with the woman, listen to her, support her as she finds her way to mercy and recovery. Without someone who understands, who agrees that a terrible thing has been done, who can help her work through her grief instead of denying that it should be there, these women may never find peace.

There is room in pro-life for people who have not always seen the truth. Dr. Bernard Nathanson, once a notorious abortionist, is a primary example. We must make room for women who have realized the evil of their "choice" and who are seeking understanding, a chance to grieve, and an opportunity to find forgiveness. There are organizations ready to help. I recommend "Women Exploited by Abortion" (P.O. Box 4082, Westmount, Quebec, H3Z 2X3) or the "Victims of Abortion Group."

It may be that the three miscarriages I have suffered have made me more sensitive to this situation. If that is so, then I thank God — good has again been resurrected from tragedy.

Chapter 14

"And what did you do?"

I've told you how uncomfortable David is with crowds. His idea of a perfect party is himself and a book. Yet ironically, his experiences of the last months have made him a much-in-demand speaker with many pro-life groups.

Every time my husband gets an invitation to speak to a group, his first reaction is "No! Not again." He hates the attention; he hates being considered a hero. Yet we both realize that David's story can help in the fight against abortion.

That's the same reason that I agreed to write this book. Basically, the entire Packer family would be very content to live quiet lives in our comfortable little home in New Toronto. But we cannot ignore the good that we might do for a cause that is one of the most important in the world — saving the lives of unborn children.

As I said before, if this book can change one person's mind about abortion, if it can spur just a few people to more involvement in this fight to save children, it will have been worth the effort, the energy, and the difficulty I face as I let strangers have a long look into my life, and the lives of my family.

David feels the same way. He may lose hours and hours of sleep over it, after he agrees to speak somewhere, and he will shake all the way to and from the podium, but he knows that good may come out of it. I guess, in a different way, speaking in public is another matter of conscience for David. He knows it's something he's supposed to do, something that is good for the cause in which he believes, something that might make a difference for the children — something God would want him to do.

So, he stands, sweating and shaking — but still smiling — and tells his story.

I want to include some excerpts from one of his recent talks in this chapter. That night, he told his audience that, "we've probably come as far down as any society has ever come.

"The medical fact, and it's not controversial in any way, is that an unborn child is a human being in every way. The matter is resolved.

"Unfortunately, all the best elements in our society continue to tell us that the earth is flat — that it's OK to kill these people and put them in garbage bags.

"All the way through history, the one sacred person has been the unborn child. Any woman convicted of a capital crime, until now, could plead, and say, 'I'm pregnant.' And that was full stop. She couldn't be executed, at least until her child was born. And no one thought anything about that, because that's the way life is.

"You can't be a policeman too long before you notice the oddest things, at least where unborn children and babies are concerned. At least twice a month, I go to some unknown site, it might be in a bar, and I get there, and everyone will be throwing chairs and tables at each other. And then you hear a lady's voice, and she says, 'My child! Watch out!' And everyone would stop fighting, and the lady would scurry around, pick up the kid, and everyone would start throwing tables and chairs again.

"There's this profound and unquestioned idea that what matters most, in our society, is the baby. People do extraordinary things when babies are trapped in buildings in fires, for example. The most miserable, hateful, swinish person will risk his or her life to get the child out, and I think it's just built into our nature to do that.

"So, we're in an incredible situation here. Medical science tells us very clearly that life begins at conception. And we're killing 4,000 children every day in North America.

"I'm not smart enough to be able to square those two things, to make it seem right.

"If I'm a Christian, I simply cannot stand by while human beings are being slaughtered. And this has got me into hot water with my employer.

"I can't stand by and believe it's OK when everything I've ever read tells me it's just plain murder. You see, police officers encounter occasionally a nebulous figure called a contract killer. They even make movies out of these guys. A contract killer, basically, drifts up from Detroit, kills your granny for four hundred bucks, and drifts back to Detroit.

"And it occurs to me that when a woman pays a stranger four hundred dollars to enter her womb and kill her child, it's just a hit. It's just a contract killing. It's no different.

"And it's preposterous to me to ask a police officer, or anyone else, to guard a place where this kind of contract killing happens twenty times a day. See, if I pay someone to kill my child 12 weeks after it's born, that's murder. If I pay that same person to kill my child 12 weeks after conception, that's just business.

"I'm not sure how a society can stand if it's this rotten.

"I've always found it relatively ludicrous, if basically harmless, when we worship Mammon, which just means crass materialism. I don't believe it, but we'll listen to all this stuff and we'll buy all this junk, and it's not a bad game. But at the end of the day, nothing is really lost, you're just 10 grand in debt, and the thing's in your driveway rusting out. But that's how life is.

"But our society appears to have gone back to worship Baal. It's worshipping the killing of its babies, the best part of it."

Later in his address, my husband talked about the issue that got him into the situation we're in — the question of conscience. He utterly rejects the idea that he is some sort of expert on the subject, but he told his audience:

"Why my face is staring out of newspapers occasionally is because, apparently, I've become the conscience of a nation. I didn't even want to be the conscience of Etobicoke.

"But apparently this is what I am. So I'll tell you something about conscience. The first thing is, your conscience never urges you to spend two weeks in Barbados. You don't lie awake at night, thinking, 'Lord, I don't want to do it, but OK, I'll go lie on the beach, and I'll drink those little drinks with the umbrellas in. I'll do it for you.'

"Conscience invariably tells you to do something you don't want to do, something which is going to disturb your life, disturb the lives of your family, and is a general pain. You just want someone else to do it. You want to say, 'Look, there are five D. Packers in the book, you must have the wrong one.'

"But your conscience says, basically, 'Listen. You know the facts, you know they're babies,

136

you know they're people. You don't believe any of this gibberish all these lunatics are putting forward. You're the police officer that they're telling to go guard the place where they're killing these kids, for money, every day. So what are you going to do about it?'

"And probably like most of you, my initial answer is 'Sure. I'll do what they want. I'll feel rotten, but everyone else is doing it. All the other Catholic policemen are doing it.' And at that time, I wasn't even a Catholic. So it's not the worst thing in the world, is it?

"So I did it once, and it was the worst thing in the world. There's nothing worse. There's nothing worse than sitting outside a place, as the highest representative of law and order, and seeing people go into that place, and knowing that the child inside them is going to be ripped apart in all its innocence.

"We don't kill our murderers any more. But we kill our children.

"So I did try it, but I couldn't do it. I couldn't be that rotten."

When David speaks to groups, he's not terribly concerned about telling his own story. He'll use anecdotes from his own experiences — and he tells funny stories very well — but he is much more interested in making people aware of the larger picture, the nation-wide horror story that is being carried out, in reality, every day in this land — and of the part they play, actively or passively, in it.

Recently, he made the point of how slippery the slope really may become, through this example:

"If they decide, when the old Blue Jays stadium is no longer needed, next year, if they decide that they want to kill old people, or black

137

people, or left-handed people, or priest people, or Catholic people or people with receding hair-lines and sticky-out eyes, they'll crowd all of these people into this concentration camp of theirs, the old Blue Jays stadium, and the Metro Police will guard the place, while they kill these people."

He told the group, "You have to be in the pro-life movement for about eight minutes before you realize that the first casualty in all of this is reason. Reason has to be killed before anyone else can be killed. And there's no reason left.

"I find it very hard, whenever I speak to any-one, to keep my patience. I don't think I'm a par-ticularly smart guy. The Roman Catholic Church, for the past two thousand years, has told us ev-erything we need to know about abortion. And belatedly, twentieth century science and medicine has utterly vindicated what the Church has been saying all along about the unborn child.

"But when I talk to people, and they're duti-fully quiet, and studious, the odd person either taking notes or doing a shopping list, I wonder why really they're not doing too much. And, of course, the question is, why am I not doing too much? Because we all know how dangerous it is when we start looking at other people and say, 'Why aren't you doing something?'

"In fact, what we're asking is, why am I not doing something?

"Now all I did was ask a guy in private if I could do another detail. If he'd said 'Yes,' it's ex-tremely unlikely you would have asked me to speak here today.

"Suddenly, I find people shoving microphones in my face and taking photographs. And sud-denly, I'm touted as some kind of expert with a corner on conscience. And I'm expected to tell everyone what they should be doing, what all the answers are.

"What all of you have to come to grips with is, you're going to die. I'm sorry to have to break it to you, but you're going to die. You're going to be dead. One day.

"A lawyer will tell you that, once in a while, a witness in a witness box, in court, is driven into a corner. It's happened to me several times. The lawyer is there. He's saying, 'Officer, I understand that the knife was on the bed and my client was standing there and the person was lying there dead. But did you see the knife in my client's hand?'

"And I say something stupid like, 'Well, not exactly, but he's the only person in the room. There's a person, a knife and someone dead.'

"And the lawyer says, 'No, no. Listen to my words, officer. Did you see the knife in my client's hand. Yes or no?'

"And I say, 'Uh, well….no.'

"And he says, 'Thank you, thank you very much. It only took twenty minutes, thank you.'

"And my point is, that when you die, you're going to have to give an account of your life. You're going to be in a corner, like no lawyer could ever drive you into. And if you say, 'Well, I read the books. I went on a march once, and it was raining. Oh, it was terrible. And I caught a cold and I felt terrible,' God is going to say to you, 'Yes, excuse me, but what did you do? What did you do to save your unborn brothers and sisters?'

"'Well, to reiterate, it was cold and blustery and the sign was falling down, and it hit me once, and it was terrible….'

"And God is going to say, 'Listen. Just answer the question. What did you do?'

"And you can say, 'Well, I wrote a letter to my M.P.'

"God's going to say, 'I know that. Get on with it. What did you do?'

"'I signed a petition.'

"God's going to say, 'Don't waste my time. There are lots of people queuing up, here. What did you do?'

"And you're going to end up saying, 'Well, I guess I didn't do a heck of a lot.'

"He's going to say, 'Did you know? Did you know of this slaughter of 4,000 people every day, just in North America?'

"'Yes.'

"'Did it disturb you?'

"'Oh, terribly!'

"'Did you tell people?'

"'Oh, yes, I did, yes.'

"'But what did you do to save them?'

"'Well, what could I do?'

"And this is what goes through my mind. What do I say on my judgment day to my God? So far, I can say I refused to go along with it. That's all I did, I refused to go along with it. Which isn't that much, really.

"I am going to do something. And my conscience is going to drive me to do it. My faith in God, my knowledge of the humanity of the unborn child, will be balanced against my earthly desires of a house in Mississauga and a Buick. And I hope that the balance will come down where I give up that Buick and that house, to do what's right.

"See, I can't stand here and tell you guys what you should do. Firstly, it's extremely presumptuous, secondly, I don't know you, your circumstances or how you think. But I'll tell you — each one of you has to ask yourself what you should do.

"Because if there's one thing which is abundantly clear, it's this: Your conscience will always give you an answer. And almost certainly you won't like the answer. I didn't. I hated the answer.

"And when you've decided what you're drawn to do, you have to do it. Because your soul is at stake.

"I'm not going to ask any of you to do anything specific. But I'd just like to ask you to think about where our society's going. I'd like you to think about what your ambitions are in life. I'd like you to ask yourself what you can do before your lifestyle is in danger, to help your unborn brothers and sisters.

"Then I'd like you to do whatever it is. Don't tell anyone, and don't work it out on paper. Don't sit down and think, 'If I do this, then I'll get this publicity... but I might lose my job... but maybe I could save this person... and my great-uncle will disinherit me... but so what, he doesn't have a nickle...'

"Don't bother counting the cost all that much. Because if you do, you're just going to come away extremely discouraged. And in all likelihood you won't do anything.

"And if you don't do anything, 4,000 people, on Monday, 4,000 beautiful people, happy and snug in their Mom's tummy right now, are going to be killed. This wonderful life that we love so much, they're never going to experience. They're going to miss out on all the good things that we take for granted.

"And at the end of your life, you're going to have to answer some pretty tough questions."

******

American Congressman Henry Hyde has issued the same challenge in these terms:

"When the time comes, as it surely will, when we face that awesome moment, the final judgment — I've often thought, as Fulton Sheen wrote, that it is a terrible moment of loneliness. You have no advocates, you are there alone standing before God — and a terror will rip your soul like nothing you can imagine. But I really think that those in the pro-life movement will not be alone. I think that there'll be a chorus of voices that have never been heard in this world, but are heard beautifully and clearly in the next world — and they will plead for everyone who has been in this movement. They will say to God, 'Spare him, because he loves us,' and God will look at you and say not, 'Did you succeed?', but 'Did you try?'"

Chapter 15

We're not going to quit

So where are we now? In this chapter, I want to answer that question in regard to David, to myself, and concerning the ongoing abortion tragedy in general.

David describes himself as being "in the penalty box." He's been handed the sort of assignment that the Metropolitan Toronto Police Department gives officers it would prefer not to have around at all — a desk job in a backwater office.

He's very clearly seen as an embarassment by the higher-ups at the department. And that embarassment is augmented by several factors: he won't quit, and they can't finally fire him until the official procedural process of appeal is over (and not even then, should he win). He also won't shut up. He continues to accept invitations to speak, and when he does, he tells it straight, just the way he sees it.

I'm very proud of him.

David Packer is also not going to go away, as far as opposition to abortion is concerned. As you have read in the last chapter, my husband has committed himself to doing as much he can to halt the horror of killing babies. I'm not even sure what his next step will be, but I know he's not going to stop fighting, and I know that he has no desire to take any easy way out.

I would say that David is more committed to this than he has ever been, much more, even, than he was on the day, a year and a half ago, when he walked into 14 Division to refuse to do duty at the Morgentaler abortuary. The courage he found then has grown in him, by the grace of God, ever since that pivotal day.

He's not going to quit his job as a cop; he's not going to quit the even more important task of fighting for the lives of babies who are being killed, 4,000 a day, on this continent alone.

******

Anne Packer is also not going to quit.

I've started to take a more active role outside the Morgentaler abortion "clinic." I now take my turn behind the building, trying to talk to the people who are going into the place.

When someone is about to enter the abortuary, we approach them, and I say, "Please, if you're going to go in there, please talk to us first. We'll help you. We'll do anything. Whatever the problem is, we'll help you."

But we're very straight with them. We also say, very plainly, "If you go in there, they're going to kill your baby."

I'm not nasty, but I'm not going to sugar-coat the horrible truth. I won't avoid mentioning the baby, because the baby's important. But I think that if you want to save that baby, you have to let the mother know that you care about her, too.

And I think you'll realize from what I have said about my miscarriages that this is not just a ploy on my part. I genuinely care about both of those people, child and mother. She is important. God loves her, too, and there's a baby inside of her, and you have to let her know that you love her and will care about her.

144

It's a terribly sad place to be, outside the clinic. One day I watched a girl go into the abortuary. She looked as if she were about 15 years old. She had a young boy with her, and he would not even look at me.

But she looked at me. Her eyes were utterly filled with fear and desperation.

I thought, "Lord, look at this person carrying this baby in there. She's probably scared to death, I know she is. She's just terrified. And maybe she's afraid her mom and dad will find out." What a reason for killing a baby — because your parents might find out.

Tell me — how many victims were there, that day, in that one case, at the Morgentaler abortuary?

I don't know if she heard me or not, but I called to her. I told her, "Your baby's depending on you."

It may sound harsh, but I was giving her the opportunity at the last minute to change her mind. She can never say that there was no one there to help her. I have talked to people who have had abortions who have told me, "if someone had said those things to me as I went in to have the abortion, I think I would have turned around and gone home." There's always that last hope.

And when women are coming out from the clinic, I'm there to say, "If there's anything we can do to help you in the future, here's a card with our number on it. Please call us."

When they come out, they look very sad, and very, very shaken, and I want them to know that the pro-life movement loves them. That's a very important distinction — we hate abortion, but we love people, no matter what they have done.

If we didn't love people, we wouldn't care as much about the smallest people, those who are being killed.

That's why there's room in pro-life for anyone who has been involved in abortion in any way, but who has come to see the truth.

I also talk to the people who work at the abortuary. I don't know where I get this boldness from, because I'm not like that, I really am not.

But, not long ago, I went up to the security guard and I said, "Why don't you join us. Why don't you stop helping them to do all the killing that is going on in there?"

When one of the doctors came out, I asked, "Why don't you stop the killing and be a healer for a change?"

There are escorts for the women who come for abortions, and I say to them, "You're working in a place where they're killing babies. Women don't kill children — they nurture and protect them. What you're doing is wrong. Why don't you join us?"

There was a man delivering equipment there. I showed him a picture of what the babies looked like, and I said, "With that equipment, you help that man in there kill children. Did you know that? What would your family think. What will they think when this is over and they know that you are a part of this?"

I know it's important for us to be there, to give the opportunity to all those involved to see the truth. But it can be a very difficult place to be, and you don't get much positive response.

When the first girl I mentioned walked in, I started crying. I felt as if I had failed, even though, intellectually, I know that I haven't. I've done the best that I can. And I'm there.

But emotionally, it's really difficult. It tears you apart.

You really can't allow yourself to feel like a failure. God gave every person free will, and we have to make our own choices. What's gut-wrenching to me is that this free will involves killing someone who's so innocent and helpless. The baby can't do a damned thing. It's horrible.

The thought of anybody hurting a child is horrific, and killing a baby like that is just terrible.

You just do the best you can. At least, you tried. You were there. At least, you spoke.

******

I am never sure what I think about the future of the whole picture concerning this ongoing holocaust — in Canada, in North America, around the world. I'm torn between my natural optimism — and any mother of five kids just has to be an optimist! — and the reality of what continues to go on, completely unchecked.

When the government of Canada voted on abortion legislation earlier this summer, I thought I saw a glimmer of hope. Every motion was lost — which left this country with absolutely no law that controls abortion — but the one that came closest to passing was the pro-life amendment. That indicates some hope, but is it enough? I really am not sure.

Sadly, the record shows that every female Member of Parliament who was present on July 28 voted against the pro-life motion. That is a strong indication of the confusion that exists between the issue of women's rights and abortion. I'm a feminist — I believe in equal rights for women.

It was only recently that I realized that I truly am a feminist. It makes me very angry to live in a society that cares so little for women. They're all so keen on letting women abort themselves, like it's some kind of liberating experience. That's not liberation — that's bondage.

Feminism is being used. Women are being used. Abortion has nothing to do with feminism, abortion has everything to do with population control. I think when the history of this time is written, it will be shown that the people who are the movers and shakers are trying to control population growth, especially in Third World countries.

It may sound bizarre at first, but I believe they have started it in this country, and on this continent, in an attempt to influence the people in the Third World to do what we do, just as they started contraception here and then exported it.

Fortunately, the people in the Third World don't pay too much attention, thank God. They value their children. The rate of abortion in Third World countries is very low compared to what Planned Parenthood and other such organizations would like to see.

I think women are being used and abused terribly. I think if women knew what abortion is about, many would not be persuaded to kill their babies. Some are aware of what they're doing, but I've read too many stories of women who really did not know the facts. Women are being used, and that should make feminists angry. Instead, a large number of feminist leaders collaborate with the abortionists.

Linking abortion with feminist rights is one of the most devilish pieces of successful propaganda this world will ever see. I pray that women will realize they are being duped.

And that's one of the reasons it makes me especially sad to see that every woman in Canada's national government voted against the pro-life amendment on abortion.

Nonetheless, that amendment attracted the most support. At times, when I think about that, I begin to feel hope. The other half of the time, I remain convinced that, unless more is done to fight the evil, the killing is not going to stop.

One thing is immediately certain — as I write this, there is an election underway in Canada. Abortion is definitely going to be an election issue.

There's also the unlikely prospect that the Supreme Court of Canada will rule that an unborn child is a child from the very beginning. But I'm not holding my breath on that one — neither the Supreme Court nor the recent federal governments have been at all kind to unborn children. A lot of responsibility for what is going on must rest right there, at the very highest levels in the land.

****

On the whole, David and I are convinced that the solution to this situation is not going to come through traditional, political activity. I'm becoming convinced — and so is my husband — that the only future for us is civil disobedience. I'm afraid that we may well find ourselves spending time in jail.

Civil disobedience may involve things like sitting down outside the "clinic", and other places where abortions are being done; it may involve chaining ourselves to the entrance way (an act for which other pro-life supporters have been arrested and charged).

In the United States, there are pro-life activists in jail for years because they have destroyed abortion equipment. To me, they are heroes of the cause.

We're coming to believe that visible, civil disobedience is the only alternative. People — the whole of society — have to be confronted with this pervasive evil. If it's not stopped now, it will grow even further. In the future, this time of ours will be looked on as the most barbaric time in human history.

Other "expendable" people are already dying — unwanted children who are born with birth defects are left to die in our hospitals. The list of the expendables will grow, and grow, to include the old and the infirm (and don't forget, probably we will all be old and possibly infirm, not too many years from now).

Who knows who else may be considered expendable, in the years to come, if this trend toward destroying the unwanted is not stopped now?

It seems to me that we can find our example in this in a very strange place indeed: if Henry Morgentaler can go to jail for the right to kill, we can go to jail to stop the killing. It's going to take some kind of major revolution to stop what's going on.

Some people ask me why David and I would even consider going to jail. My only answer is, if we take that route, we will take it because it is what we should be doing, what Jesus wants us to do. I don't want to stand before Jesus Christ, and be ashamed.

There is a very great danger of apathy, of being content with less than success, in pro-life. It's easy to believe that we're doing all we can, but this is so far from the truth.

If we discovered that some group of adults was being killed — handicapped people, or Baptists, or some other identifiable group — we would not be content to write letters and stage marches. We would be fools if we did.

No, it would take something much more direct, and we'd be willing to do that something to save lives.

Sometimes, I wonder if even those of us in pro-life really believe the babies who are dying are human beings. Our responses seem so inadequate, so often. When they look back on us, in the future, won't they ask, "Why didn't you do something? Why didn't you stop it?"

How will we answer?

Chapter Sixteen

Abortion must stop, now!

You've read the story of David and Anne Packer. You know the things that have happened to us, the strange drama that unfolded around a man who was hoping for nothing more than to avoid just exactly that kind of confrontation.

In the preceding chapter, I gave you a bit of a glimpse into where David and I may be going from here.

Now: what about you?

Throughout this book, I've talked a lot about abortion. You may have encountered facts about this terrible curse that you have never heard before. You may have heard some ideas that are new to you.

Or, it may be that all the facts and figures are old hat to you.

Either way, I ask again: what about you?

******

It's been stated in several places in this book that 4,000 human beings are being slaughtered, every day, in North America. In this chapter, I want to share a few more of the facts with you.

Are you aware that, at the time I write this book, there is absolutely no abortion law in Canada? Previously, we had a weak law that was very loosely interpreted and hardly at all enforced. I'm not convinced the situation was much better then.

But if it could have become worse, it has. The Supreme Court of Canada has thrown out the previous law as unconstitutional. That means, until a new law comes into place, anything goes.

Morgentaler is completely free to operate free-standing aborturaries, at this point in time.

The federal government engaged in a lengthy debate over new abortion legislation. The only result was that there was no result. Every motion presented in the House of Commons was defeated.

The strongest vote came in favor of the pro-life amendment. While it, too, was defeated, that tells us there may be some cause for hope.

Since the matter will undoubtedly come up again in Parliament, this seems to me to be a very good time for anyone concerned about the evil of abortion. Contacting your Member of Parliament could make a difference.

What about you? Will you do that much?

******

Early in the book, I mentioned some of the first things I did when I began to be aware of the abortion issue. At the very beginning, I read everything I could find about abortion, about the development of a baby, and about what was being done to stop the killing of children.

What about you? If you are new to this entire issue, are you willing to spend some of your time simply educating yourself? There are many books and educational materials available through the offices of local pro-life groups. Take the time to find out what really is going on.

But don't stop there.

******

As I said earlier, as well, my first pro-life act was to write a letter to the editor of my local newspaper.

I would now insist that writing letters is not nearly enough. But it is a start. Again, it is necessary to keep the public reminded of the ongoing tragedy, and reminded, as well, that pro-life activists are not going to go away.

When you write to the newspaper, be prepared to be criticized. You may draw nasty letters in response. You may have phone calls to your house.

But someone may read that letter and think for a few minutes about abortion and how it touches them. Even if you "convert" no one, your first letter might be seen as your initiation into the battle.   So what about you? Are you willing to declare yourself, to put your reputation on the line, to be considered a pro-life fanatic? What about you?

****

I have mentioned a number of pro-life organizations which are actively working toward the ending of the abortion holocaust. I'm especially grateful for the work of Campaign Life Coalition.

These groups need volunteer workers and financial donations, so they may keep up the work they are doing. That work must not only be maintained, it must be increased if we are to make a difference.

What about you? Will you join one or more pro-life organizations, and give some of your time, your energy, and your money to help save the lives of children who will die if we cannot find some way to stop the killing?

****

David and I are seriously considering the use of civil disobedience as a method of serving the cause of unborn children. I urge you to ask yourselves some hard questions about such actions, as well.

I'm not suggesting that this is something everyone will be called to. Instead, to quote my husband, listen to your conscience.

But we warn you — your conscience is probably going to tell you to do things you may not want to do. But they will be the right things to do; they may be hard, but they will be what God wants you to do.

One thing is certain — whatever form your next step takes, from writing letters to the editor to chaining yourself to an abortuary fence, your conscience, if you are listening, will tell you to become involved in the struggle to stop abortion in this country.

******

In this country, at least 180 children are killed by abortion every day. That's one Canadian life taken by violence every eight minutes.

These babies are killed by suction machines, which rip them apart; they are killed by salt poisoning, which burns them; they are killed by drugs which cause premature delivery — prostaglandin, which I wrote about in the earliest chapters of this book — and often delivered alive, and left to die; they are aborted by caesarean section, the same operation that delivers full-term, "wanted babies" — but the aborted babies are left to die.

All of these torturous methods of killing unborn children are completely legal in Canada. Most or all of them will be used today, to end the lives of Canadian children.

What are you going to do about it?

We must do something. As the argument goes on, as we write and discuss and listen to speakers, babies are dying.

Abortion must stop. It must stop, now.

Chapter Seventeen

Friends of the unborn children

As I have stated before, David and I have received an incredible amount of support from pro-life people from around the world. This chapter simply consists of letters from people of conscience, letters than have meant an enormous amount to David and to me. To each person who took the time to write, I say thank you, and God bless you.

Many of the letters came from people who are intensely involved in the pro-life movement, such as this one, from Adelle Nathanson:

"Dear Constable Packer,

"When I was last in Toronto someone told me that you were in the audience. I wanted very much to shake your hand at that time but events and people swept me out of the hall and back to the hotel without allowing me to do so. I deeply regret missing that chance, but hope that this letter will somewhat help to bridge that lost opportunity.

"I had wanted at that time to tell you personally your courageous action has placed you among those very few in our countries who are willing to place their lives, careers, and families on the line for their beliefs. Each weekend my husband and I are in a different city, and Bernard speaks to yet another group of people who are interested in vital life issues. He never misses an opportunity to talk about you by name and your courageous action, as well as those very few others who stand beside you, placing their bodies and their lives between the abortophiles and the babies.

"I wish you all the strength in the world and my continuing gratitude for the sterling example that you set for the rest of us who struggle in defense of those most defenseless among us — the unborn.

"Faithfully,
"Adelle Nathanson"

*****

Adelle Nathanson referred in her letter to others who have placed much on the line in the fight against abortion. Some, both in Canada and in the United States, have done time in jail for their active opposition to the slaughter of unborn children. Many of these have been charged after they have destroyed abortion machines. One such man wrote to us from British Columbia:

"Dear David,
"Just a brief note to let you know how much we admire you for the stand you have taken. In these times it is becoming rarer and rarer that people stand for what they know to be right. Please give our regards to your wife and family as well. It takes a lot of support to be in the kind of fight you are in and I am sure that they are contributing a great deal. Thank you again.

"Yours for life,
"Jim Demers and family, Nelson, British Columbia"

*****

158

Letters from "prisoners of conscience" were especially touching for us. One of the most heroic, in my opinion, is Joan Andrews who spent two years and seven months in prison for unplugging an abortion machine in Florida. She was released in October, 1988 thanks to thousands of pro-lifers who protested her unjust sentence. While still in prison she wrote to' David:

"Dear Constable Packer,

"May God bless you for your inspiring stance on behalf of truth and out of love for and in defense of the dignity of our preborn brothers and sisters. I cannot express the depths of my gratitude. Your story of faithfulness to the Lord and his little ones is being spread far and wide, and I have no doubt that our Lord will use it to change many hearts and to save many lives.

"Already, many policemen in many cities throughout the U.S.A. are being told your story as an example of the proper actions of a Christian officer. Please God, more will follow your courageous example.

"I am a prolifer in prison for trying to save the lives of little preborn babies scheduled for the slaughter. How 'nice' it would be if Christian police officers would refuse to arrest life-savers doing rescues at killing centres. We do have a former police chief, Edward Allen (now 80 years old and a godly man) doing rescues and he has likewise been arrested for his life-saving efforts. Ed wrote me that he also had heard about you and was very grateful for your actions.

"Please know that many, many people love you, support you and are praying for you and your beloved family. From all of us, and for the babies, and the Holy Christian Faith, we say

Thank you, dear David, with all our hearts.
"God bless you,
"Joan Andrews"

*****

We also heard from Michael Bray, a prisoner in New York for his pro-life activism.

"Dear Mr. Packer,
"I have had the pleasure of reading about your efforts to resist the evil of childslaughter and particularly to risk the loss of your job in doing what is right. Your courage in obeying your conscience is an encouragement to all who hear about you and your faithful wife who stands behind you.

"I trust that your example will spur others into greater action — even that sacrificial action required to defeat the evil which has been spilled over all the earth.

"During the past 28 months I have been in prison here in New York in connection with the destruction of childslaughterhouses. It is always good to hear about people like you and your honorable wife. I have also been blessed by the support of a holy wife, who has borne the strain of my imprisonment as she tends to the task of raising our three children (aged six, four and three).

"The Lord bless and keep you as you continue to stand for him and for his innocents. Please pray for us as we pray for you.
"Free in Christ,
"Michael Bray"

*****

We received letters of support from almost every source imaginable. It was not rare to receive a message like those written above on the same day as a letter from a young child. The voices of the children meant a lot. Teresa Johnson-Lillyman of Manitoba wrote:

"Dear Constable Packer,

"My name is Teresa Johnson-Lillyman and I am 11 years old. I wrote to tell you I think it is great you would not protect the abortionary (sic) and I think you deserve a medal for it.

"I disagree with abortion totally, and I think you have to be one of the most unselfish, generous, caring people there is.

"I give you full support on what you are doing and think everyone should.

"Sincerely,

"Teresa Johnson-Lillyman"

In her letter she included a hand-drawn medal. David has kept it.

*****

A Glasgow, Scotland teacher, Brian Carring, read about David's situation and told his class about us. We received a package of letters, which Brian assured us were written independently by the children. Joanne wrote:

"Dear Constable,

"I am supporting you for the protection of the unborn child. I think it is terrible cutting off the life of an unborn child. I agree with you when you said the safest place in the world should be when the baby is in the womb of its mother.

"I pray for these sick people, that they may come to their senses."

*****

Kathleen, from that same Scottish school wrote:

"I am writing to tell you that it is right about what you are saying about abortion. I think that people who abort their babies are mad because they are killing an unborn baby. The mother who aborts her child is just thinking about what she should do and not thinking about the baby's rights too.

"Whoever brought up this thing about abortion must have been evil-minded. I think that babies should be born, not killed, and something should be done about it."

*****

David, of this wonderful Scottish class, wrote:

"I am writing this letter to support you and your actions. I can assure you that my whole class feel very deeply about this diabolical act.

"The time that followed must have been very trying for you and your family. You must remember that you did the right thing, and God is on your side. You refused to guard a place where murderers go about their evil disgusting business. Killing live babies is disgusting!

"The babies are alive! They can move in the womb, can clench a fist, but still we go on with this barbaric ritual. We are all behind you, 100 per cent."

*****

This Scottish class was not the only group of students to write, voicing their support for David and his action. We received two packages of letters from St. Maurice school in Winnipeg, Manitoba.

Anil wrote:

"Dearest Constable Packer,

"I agree with you totally about how wrong abortion is. It is plain murder. I am real sorry that you lost your job, but God will reward you for what you have done, in heaven. I wish you and your family the best of luck, and I will remember you in my prayers."

*****

Ryan, from the same school, wrote a letter that was short and to the point:

"Dear sir,

"You did the right thing. Sorry about your job, but I'm with you all the way. Hope things get better."

*****

Ian, also from St. Maurice, wrote:

"I totally agree with your decision on abortion. Hopefully, you will get your job back, if not I hope that God will help you with a new job. Thank you for your decision."

*****

Another package of letters arrived from the grade six class at Saint John Brebeuf School in Winnipeg. Mark wrote:

"I think you have done the right thing, when you said no. You probably felt scared, but now, you should feel good!"

Elizabeth, from the same class, wrote:

"I wrote to thank you for risking your job to save other human beings from being murdered. If my daddy did this, I would tell him I loved him. I don't know how a mother could kill her child."

The next two letters were especially powerful. Both were from mothers, but mothers in very different circumstances. From Pittsburgh, a woman wrote:

"God bless you for your stand against abortion. I pray that more law enforcement officers will take the same stand. As the mother of ten, I had unwanted and inconvenient pregnancies, but believe me, I never had an unwanted baby. One look was all it took — one look at that precious infant."

But one of the most powerful letters was from a California woman who never had the chance to look at her healthy new-born.

"Dear Officer Packer,

"I think it took a lot of guts to stand up for your beliefs. I wouldn't guard an abortion clinic either! I'm the victim of an abortion, one done when I wasn't told how far along I was, that I had a baby within me and that I had other options besides killing my child. My healing from my abortion has been the most difficult trauma in my life, next to the rape that caused my pregnancy.

"You know, people tell me I had every right to abort my little girl, but I don't feel any better when I hear that. The man who raped me was never punished, but my child was. What those clinics are doing is wrong. They lie, they don't tell you all of the facts and they pressure girls to have abortions. They make a lot of money doing it, too!

"I hope there will be more policemen like you. And I also hope someday abortion will be made illegal again. Adoption is such a better option. If I had known, my daughter would have been adopted and she'd be alive."

*****

We received many letters from ministers and priests from many different churches. It is encouraging to know that, on this issue, Christians from all denominations are involved. Pastor Fred Vaughn, of Beulah Baptist Church in Toronto, wrote:

"Dear David and Mrs. Packer,

"I thank God for the courageous stand you have taken in refusing to guard the illegal death house at Harbord Street. Even though the judgement was disappointing, I know you will win your appeal and you will give courage to many others to stand for righteousness.

"May God intervene to stop the terrible killing of precious babies. We are praying for you and for your family in these difficult days."

*****

Anglican minister Rev. Larry Winslow, of Thessalon, Ontario, wrote:

"There are many of us here in northern Ontario who not only support your stand but also admire you for your courage in standing up for righteousness.

"This society, most especially its leaders, is trying to force you into defending the place of business of those who are committing the unmitigated murder of innocent, unborn human beings. Ironic, isn't it."

*****

Dr. Olga Fairfax, of Methodists United for Life, in the U.S., wrote:

"Methodists United for Life salutes you for your courage, bravery and guts. Thank God there is still one policeman defending innocent, pre-born babies' lives."

*****

Sister Carmelita Solomon, C.S.M., of Prince Edward Island, wrote:

"I hail you as a brave hero for refusing to guard the Morgentaler clinic. I strongly support your efforts to uphold the rights of the unborn."

*****

Rev. Dan Reinhardt, of Hillcrest Evangelical Church in Medicine Hat, Alberta, wrote:

"I applaud you for your courage and your commitment to the principles that you firmly believe in, even if it means putting your job on the line. It is so encouraging to see different people beginning to stand up for life here in Canada. "

*****

We received a copy of a letter sent from Rev. Robert Bulbrook, of Holy Family Roman Catholic Church in Hanover, Ontario, to Police Chief Jack Marks. The letter said:

"It is reported that St. Thomas More said, 'I am the king's good servant, but God's first.' I suppose that in each generation there will be those who are martyred to authority.

"I certainly hope that the charges against Constable Packer will be dropped, not only because it is a matter of conscience but because I fear the perversion of the law when our police officers can be ordered to defend illegal activities.

"Except for the issue, I cannot see the difference between police protection of illegal abortion clinics and the protection of the offices of a drug ring because the proprietor had been clever enough to tie things up in court. The examples could go on and on.

"I will be praying not only for Constable Packer but for you. The position of leadership is a great weight but even that weight can never be held up with the words, 'I was only following orders.' One police state defending itself that way is enough for one century."

*****

Rev. Cal MacInnis, of St. James Presbyterian Church, Newcastle, New Brunswick, wrote:

"I realize that you face an uncertain future and that the result of your superior's judgement is quite unpredictable, but I know you have a lot of supporters 'out there.' All of us who do agree that the dictates of conscience demand resistance to an operation which is outside the law. It is unconscionable that any police force should be guarding an illegal operation so that it can operate freely.

"Though the cost may be high for you, it is not so high that God cannot match or better it!"

*****

We received letters from other pro-life supporters who have lost their jobs because of their stands, or who are prepared to do so. A nursing student from Peterborough, Ontario wrote:

"I am a nineteen-year-old woman currently enrolled at Sir Sanford Fleming College in Peterborough. I am entering my second year of the Nursing program. The issue of abortion has been brought up numerous times during my classes in the past, only to be brushed aside by most of the teachers. Quite often it had been me who brought it up. I was told by many of my fellow students to 'watch myself' around the teachers, because if they were of the opposite opinion to me, they could fail me if they wanted to.

"I am a strong anti-abortioner, and being told this angered me. I greatly admire your stand against the guarding of the abortion clinic in Toronto. As a future nurse, I often wonder if I could ever be threatened with dismissal from a job if I refuse to assist with performing an abortion. If that were to happen, I guess I would be job-hunting because, like you, I cannot conscientiously support the legal human slaughter in Canada.

"Thank you for doing something most people haven't got the guts to do. You have my and my family's support."

*****

Joseph P. Wall, of Philadelphia, knows what it is like to put your livelihood on the line. He wrote:

"You have, I assure you, the love and admiration of pro-lifers everywhere for your outstanding act of moral courage. Please God, public officials at all levels would follow your example and refuse to enforce immoral, and therefore nonexistent, laws.

"I know from my own conversations with many individual officers, in the course of eleven years of picketing and prayer vigils, they do not like this kind of duty but so far have been unwilling to make a 'public' protest. 'I have to do it, I have a wife and kids to support,' or some variant, is the usual response.

"I can readily sympathize with this, having been fired from my own city government job as an auditor, for my pro-life activity. Sooner or later, though, all of us will have to make a decision as to which side we are on, the police along with everyone else. There is no middle ground, the illusion that there is is rapidly disappearing.

"I have been involved with the pro-life movement for almost 18 years now, having helped organize our local S.E. Pennsylvania group. Four years ago, it became apparent to me (and to others) that our pro-life efforts, however well-intentioned, simply weren't working, weren't doing the job. The killing was still going on, as massively as ever. We had educated all we were ever going to without access to the mass media, our lobbying efforts were no longer bearing fruit, the politicians had learned how to handle the issue with minimum damage. We could either reconcile ourselves to living with the holocaust, trying to save a handful of lives through sidewalk counselling and the like, or we could strike out in a different direction, that of massive (eventually, we hope) non-violent civil resistance.

"And so, small groups began to go to the free-standing clinics and sitting-in (we call them rescues, now), placing our bodies between the abortionist's deadly weapon and the little children he sought to kill. What followed are arrests, beatings and increasingly harsh prison sentences. We hope and pray we shall be able to arouse the conscience of the community, that we will be joined by hundreds, then thousands, to the point where the authorities will no longer be able to treat this as a simple criminal matter, but will have to involve the political process. This is what happened during the Black civil rights revolution here in the U.S. during the sixties. We hope to be able to replicate their success, and God willing, we shall do so."

*****

Joe Wall is right — there is much to do, and we in the pro-life movement must look at new ways of saving unborn lives. But one thing our mail showed us is that there are a lot of people out there who are willing to get involved. This delightful letter came from Niagara Falls, Ontario:

"Dear Mr. and Mrs. Packer and family,

"Hi! I hope that you are all doing well and still have lots of energy. I am keeping you in my prayers and am with you all the way in this fight for life. You are a fine example to all pro-lifers. You are a very courageous family, definitely a great sign from God! People like you are what keeps the pro-life movement growing and running strong. Thank you for reassuring me and giving me a boost by letting me know that there are great people like you in the world.

"Words can't express the feelings of happiness and strength you have filled me with. You will definitely get your reward in heaven.

"God bless you,

"Nicole Marie Savoie"

*****

The next letter was not sent to us. It was a letter to the editor of the police association newsletter in Toronto. But it gave us strength and encouragement, as you might guess.

"Dear editor,

"I am writing this letter to the Association in hope of helping out an officer who is being penalized as a result of his personal religious convictions. It seems to me that religion plays an important part in the lives of those who uphold the law.

"We are required to swear on the bible every time we give evidence in court. We are required to take an oath of office and we are required to enforce laws that are basically based on the laws of God expressed in the bible. Any officer who calls himself a Christian knows that God's law comes first.

"The Department has made great gains as of late with respect to allowing its employees to practice their individual religions. I am referring, of course, to the Sikh members of the Department being allowed to wear their religious attire. A move that I, for one, applaud.

"I am shocked at the way the Department is being two-faced about religion. On the one hand they expect that our religious convictions will force us to tell the truth on the stand and that our oath of office will compel us to do our duty. And, on the other hand, they tell us that our own personal feelings about issues that affect our religion, such as abortion, have to take back seat to our duty. As far as Christians are concerned, abortion is a crime of horrendous magnitude. And, as I have said before, it is every Christian's responsibility to obey God's law first.

"To the officer of 14 Division — I support your efforts wholeheartedly and wish you the best of luck. To the rest of the membership, I urge you to write to the Association and express your views so that we may be heard and represented on this all-important issue. The next time someone comes up to that particular officer in 14 Division on the street and asks, 'How do you sleep at night?', I'm sure he'll be able to say 'Just fine, thanks.' What will you be able to say?

"P.C.O. Shane Turnidge"

*****

Whenever someone puts his or her job on the line, some people are going to wonder, "what about their family?" A letter from Thunder Bay, Ontario, put that into perspective.

"We thank you and commend you for the tremendous integrity and courage you have displayed by refusing guard duty at the abortuary. It is extremely difficult to find appropriate words to reflect the feelings you have stirred in us. We are deeply moved. We fully support you and are willing to help however we can.

"Someday, the history of these times will be recorded and your heroic actions will be seen as having played a very significant role. In an age of weakness and moral fuzziness, your children can be very proud that their dad has shown himself to be a man of conviction, leadership and vision.

"Your family will be in our minds and hearts,
"John Carroll and Joanne Norlund-Carroll"

*****

From British Columbia came this lovely letter:

"David, I'm just feeding my five-month-old baby. He's just learning to hold his bottle, spending more time talking to his bottle than drinking its contents. As I read the back of the Pro-life News and see your picture with your children, and read about your courageous stand against wrong, I think Praise the Lord! There are so few people who dare to stand for what is right. Keep it up!

"Not only are you doing what is right, but you are an example and hopefully a catalyst who will encourage me and the many, many others who know the right but are afraid and cautious to step out and do the right.

"Thank you and may God continue to give you the strength, courage and wisdom to do what is right.

"Christa Haverhals"

*****

We also received letters from people in the medical field. One was sent from Saskatoon, Saskatchewan:

"Having read the news report about your declining to stand guard at the 'illegal' abortion clinic of Dr. Morgentaler, I understand that you will be having to face a court trial, with a possible release from police duty.

"The Morgentaler clinic, I understand, was being operated despite the Ontario Court of Appeals conviction, and that the police were required to stand guard to protect an 'illegal practice.' If this isn't the height of inconsistency, I can't understand plain moral principles!

"Constable Packer, you have my fullest sympathy, even apart from any religious convictions, and I support your stance.

"I do hope that you will be fully exonerated and that the Toronto Police Superintendent will also undergo a change of heart!

"Dr. R.M. Baerg"

*****

The Alliance for Life is an important pro-life group, serving as the national co-ordinating organization for pro-life groups across Canada. Executive Director Anna M. Desilets wrote from Winnipeg to offer her encouragement, and that of the groups she represents.

"I have been reading the transcript of your hearing, and I wish to express to you both personally and on behalf of the 255 member groups of Alliance For Life my deepest admiration for the very difficult courageous gesture you have made in solidarity with the unborn children of our troubled age.

174

"I was deeply impressed by the clear, straightforward and very polite way in which you answered your judges. Rarely have unborn babies had such an eloquent defender! By doing your duty and following your conscience, you have done an immeasurable service to the cause of life, and of right thinking.

"Please accept our heartiest thanks for your very moral action and be assured that we remember you and your family in our prayers."

*****

This short, touching letter came from Steinbach, Manitoba:

"Dear David,
"Even if we don't know each other, we share the same job. I, too, would refuse to guard a butcher's house if told or ordered by my superiors.
"Richard Somers"

*****

Many people who wrote to David had no way of knowing our home address. Therefore, many letters were sent to the Police Department, where those charged with the duty of reading the mail had a frequent, healthy diet of pro-life sentiments. Some of those who wrote made sure other policemen saw the letters, including this one, which was copied to the Metro Police Chief.

"Dear Constable Packer,

"I would like to support and commend you on your courageous stand against guarding abortionist Morgentaler's 'House of Death.' Your refusal to compromise your conscience is an inspiration to me and my family.

"The Nuremburg War Crimes Tribunal rejected the excuse of 'following orders' as a valid defense. History will surely judge those collaborating in this present day holocaust similarly.

"Rita Roy, Sault Ste. Marie, Ontario"

*****

From Toronto, a woman wrote to share the wonderful results of a difficult decision many years ago.

"Congratulations for your stand on the abortion issue. You will never regret your decision because God watches over us always. My husband and I took a strong stand 25 years ago, and we have never regretted it. When our handicapped daughter was born, there was pressure to put her in an institution because she is crippled and blind.

"We decided to keep her with us and help her the best way we could. This year, she is in her second year in university, lives in residence and is a happy, well-adjusted girl.

"Miracles happen!"

*****

Dave and Joan Hatherly wrote, from Toronto:
"Your so-called 'insubordination' has done us proud as Canadians, humanitarians and Christians. There are many words we could use to express our heartfelt gratitude to and admiration for your brave and moral actions, but there isn't paper enough. It is to our country's shame that you are being persecuted by our own law enforcement officers.

"Thank you for showing our children that there are godly men willing to take a stand, even at personal risk, in defense of our society's smallest and most helpless victims."

*****

We received letters from almost every Canadian province, from many states in the United States, from Great Britain and from Europe. They were mailed to our home, to the Police Department, to Campaign Life Coalition and to Right to Life. They came from lawyers, doctors, professors, housewives, factory workers, teachers, children and senior citizens.

The encouragement we found in them is immeasurable. So, too, is the impact these people can have on society, if we are willing to put ourselves on the line to save the unborn children.

I close this book with one more letter, a simple, short statement from Alice Rahn, of Wisconsin. She didn't say much, but she said it all:

"Thank you for your courage to say 'No.' Would that God would give that same kind of courage to others. We need people to take that kind of stand and, with God's help, bring the killing of the little, unborn babies to an end."

Amen.